THE TAPESTRY OF TRAUMA

Transforming the Tangles of
Childhood Sexual Abuse into God's Masterpiece

ENDORSEMENTS

For those facing trauma, it's so often those terrible images that once again rob us of life and loving relationships. Which is why you need to read Donna Scott's book today. Each chapter—each colored thread she describes—offers a way out of the pain and hiding. A way upward toward love and freedom and renewal. It's practical. Wonderfully helpful. And your head will shake at the depth of her understanding and your heart will be encouraged by her words of deep healing and hope.
—**John Trent, PhD** president, StrongFamilies.com and Author of LifeMapping® and The Blessing

Warm, gentle, and nurturing, *The Tapestry of Trauma* is full of spiritual encouragement and down-to-earth psychological insight for survivors of childhood sexual abuse. Donna Scott shares candidly from her own healing journey, calling sisters to step out of shame and into hope. This book is for every Christian woman who feels like "damaged goods" and needs to be reminded of the truth of who she is in Christ and the beauty of the tapestry God is able to weave out of all the strands of her life.
—**Joy Wong Liu**, Licensed Marriage and Family Therapist

Donna beautifully weaves her journey of healing, Biblical truths, and the wisdom and experience she has

gained as a counselor to gently guide readers through the recovery process. A must read for survivors, caregivers, and anyone hoping to support someone in their journey to heal.
—**Crystal Sutherland**, author *of Journey to Heal: Seven Essential Steps of Recovery for Survivors of Childhood Sexual Abuse* and founder of Journey to Heal Ministries

Donna Scott has bravely, courageously written the words that describe the hurt shared by countless victims of sexual abuse, by sharing her personal truth of pain and shame, while bringing hope, healing, and a future for everyone who reads this inspiring, life-changing book.
—**Tonilee Adamson and Bobbye Brooks**, founders of Daily Disciples Ministries, Inc.

This book is a gentle combination of information and inspiration. By sharing her own experience of healing from childhood sexual abuse, Donna gives hope that the reader can be healed as well. Using the colors in a tapestry, Donna identifies the threads that God is weaving to make us His masterpiece, despite sexual trauma. Her tenderness with such a difficult subject shines through every chapter."
—**Kathy Haecker**, MA, LPC, Liberating Grace Christian Counseling

I know Donna Scott. Her love and care in real life is captured in this beautifully written, biblically sound, and therapeutically comforting book of help and hope. Your heart is safe within the pages of *The Tapestry of Trauma*. Opening this book will also open your heart to the masterpiece God wants to weave to bring you the "future and hope" he has for your life.
—**Pam Farrel**, co-director of Love-Wise and author of fifty-five books including coauthor of bestselling *Men Are Like Waffles, Women Are Like Spaghetti* and *Discovering Hope in the Psalms: A Creative Bible Study Experience*

Donna writes with biblical, theological, and psychological insight. Most of all, she writes with wisdom, heart, and faith. Her words speak of indescribable pain and injury, yet the message is of healing and hope, using beautiful imagery. A book for those who experienced trauma as well as for those who care about the traumatized.
—**Minoa Chang**, PhD, psychologist and professor

THE TAPESTRY OF TRAUMA

Transforming the Tangles of
Childhood Sexual Abuse into God's Masterpiece

DONNA S. SCOTT, LMFT

COPYRIGHT NOTICE

The Tapestry of Trauma: Transforming the Tangles of Childhood Sexual Abuse into God's Masterpiece

First edition. Copyright © 2022 by Donna S. Scott. The information contained in this book is the intellectual property of Donna S. Scott and is governed by United States and International copyright laws. All rights reserved. No part of this publication, either text or image, may be used for any purpose other than personal use. Therefore, reproduction, modification, storage in a retrieval system, or retransmission, in any form or by any means, electronic, mechanical, or otherwise, for reasons other than personal use, except for brief quotations for reviews or articles and promotions, is strictly prohibited without prior written permission by the publisher.

Unless otherwise indicated, all Scripture quotations are taken from the *Holy Bible*, New Living Translation, copyright © 1996, 2004, 2015 by Tyndale House Foundation. Used by permission of Tyndale House Publishers, Inc., Carol Stream, Illinois 60188. All rights reserved.

Scripture quotations marked MSG are taken from *THE MESSAGE*, copyright © 1993, 2002, 2018 by Eugene H. Peterson. Used by permission of NavPress. All rights reserved. Represented by Tyndale House Publishers, Inc.

Scripture quotations marked HCSB are taken from the Holman Christian Standard Bible®, Copyright © 1999, 2000, 2002, 2003, 2009 by Holman Bible Publishers. Used by permission. Holman Christian Standard Bible®, Holman CSB®, and HCSB® are federally registered trademarks of Holman Bible Publishers.

Unless otherwise indicated, all definitions are taken from Merriam-Webster's Online Unabridged Dictionary, https://unabridged.merriam-webster.com/. All rights reserved. Merriam-Webster Online (www.Merriam-Webster.com) is copyrighted 2021 by Merriam-Webster, Incorporated. Used by permission of Merriam-Webster, 47 Federal Street, P.O. Box 281, Inc., Springfield, MA 01102.

Cover and Interior Design: Amber Weigand-Buckley, Derinda Babcock, Deb Haggerty

Cover Illustration: Ken Weigand

Editor(s): Carrie Del Pizzo, Susan K. Stewart, Deb Haggerty
Author Represented By: AuthorizeMe Literary Agency

PUBLISHED BY: Elk Lake Publishing, Inc., 35 Dogwood Drive, Plymouth, MA 02360, 2022

Library Cataloging Data

Names: Scott, Donna S. (Donna S. Scott)

The Tapestry of Trauma: Transforming the Tangles of Childhood Sexual Abuse into God's Masterpiece / Donna S. Scott

204 p. 23cm × 15cm (9in × 6 in.)

Identifiers: ISBN-13: 978-1-64949-516-7 (paperback) | 978-1-64949-517-4 (trade paperback) | 978-1-64949-518-1 (e-book)

Key Words: Childhood Sexual Abuse Christian; Sexual Abuse Healing Book; Childhood Sexual Abuse Survivors; Childhood Trauma Healing Book; Childhood Sexual Abuse Recovery; Childhood Trauma Christian; Christian Healing Childhood Trauma Books for Women

Library of Congress Control Number: 2022934192 Nonfiction

DEDICATION

To my beloved mother, Dr. Emily Jean Ferrell, the woman who took the dark threads of abuse and turned them into the tapestry of God's masterpiece. I miss you, Mom. Rest in heaven.

TABLE OF CONTENTS

Foreword xiii

Acknowledgments xv

My Heart for You 1

Part I: Wounded by Childhood Sexual Abuse 3

Chapter 1—A New View: Discover God's Perspective . . 5

Chapter 2—Our Tapestry: Untangle the Threads 13

Chapter 3—The Red Thread of Trauma: Acknowledge the Damage 19

Chapter 4—The Brown Thread of Triggers: Understand the Survival Skills 27

Chapter 5—The Gray Thread of Shame: Realize It is Not Your Fault 39

Chapter 6—The Maroon Thread of Discouragement: Defeat the Desire to Give Up 57

Chapter 7—The Black Thread of Fear: Develop Healthy Intimacy 71

Part II: Healed in God's Tapestry 85

Chapter 8—The Green Thread of Commitment: Decide to Heal 87

Chapter 9—The Purple Thread of Perseverance: Manage Setbacks to Healing 99

Chapter 10—The Blue Thread of Hope: Reach for Your Healing 111

Chapter 11—The Gold Thread of Faith: Receive the Rewards of Healing 121

Chapter 12—The White Thread of Forgiveness: Release Anger and Receive Healing Peace 135

Chapter 13—God's Tapestry: Picture Your Healing... 151
Appendix A—Possible Symptoms of Trauma 163
Appendix B—The Armor of God 165
Endnotes 177
Resources..................................... 181

FOREWORD

In recent weeks, I have had the privilege of reading Donna Scott's book on childhood sexual abuse and its lasting traumatic effects. The book lays a strong emphasis on transformation and healing and is beautifully woven with Scripture, personal transparency, and intriguing insight from the author. I have known Donna for many years through her father and mother, Drs. H. L. and Emily Ferrell. I've seen her dedication and commitment to the cause of helping many families come out of the bondage of hurt and despair through her Christian counseling practice. For the last several years, I have had the privilege of being the Scott family Senior Pastor, thus having the opportunity to watch her serve firsthand and admire her gifted work as a Christian counselor.

This book is a personal journey and a labor of love from every fiber of Donna's soul, mind, and body. Her imagery of a tapestry is heartfelt and compelling. We know in our own lives that pulling a thread from a piece of a garment may seem easy, but once we pick on it, we are unaware of the effects that one part of thread can have on the whole garment. Just like we are unaware of the effect one thread of delitescent child abuse can have on a now coping adult. Donna's book will give the reader clear tools to help them transition into the masterpiece our Lord has called them to be from the foundation of this world. Therefore, let the words and spirit of Donna's writing minister to your deepest needs, and please allow the Holy Spirit to re-thread you into the perfect tapestry you have always been in our Lord's eyes. I highly recommend this book to be used as a ministry resource in your counseling ministry.

Godspeed and his Love,
Bishop A.B. Vines, Sr.
Senior Pastor, New Seasons Church

ACKNOWLEDGMENTS

My heart is so full as I write these words. You know the saying, "It takes a village to raise a child"? Well, I could not have completed this book without a tribe of supporters challenging me, praying for me, and encouraging me every step of the way.

To my husband, William Ronald Scott—you are the answer to my prayers for a mate. God blessed me exceedingly abundantly above all I imagined when I thought of marriage. You show me what unconditional love looks like every day. You captured my heart, and I thank God for you. I also appreciate you staying out of the room so I can write unhindered. This book is the result of your sacrifice. I love you.

To my blessings, who doctors did not expect me to have—Sharyna, DeRon, Shariana, and DeShon. Sharyna— You lifted my heart with your words of encouragement when I wanted to quit. DeRon, you shared your gift of words and helped shaped this book. Shariana, your artistic ability is the inspiration for the cover. DeShon, your hugs and prayers carried me through. I am so grateful God chose me to be your mom. I love you all.

To my parents, Dr. H. L. and Dr. E. Jean Ferrell. I am so grateful to you both for breaking generational curses and being the first in your family to live a life dedicated to God.

You not only introduced Anthony (my brother) and me to the Lord, but you also lived a life worthy of the call he has on you. You inspired your children and your grandchildren to follow and serve God because of your example. I thank God for both of you.

To my prayer partner, sister, and friend, Diane Hayes, you prayed me through my tears and fears. You gifted me with a tapestry as a sign of confidence and encouragement I would get this book written. Every word was written with the tapestry at my back or on my lap. Thank you for believing in me and supporting me. I am so glad we get to do life together.

To my therapist partner and beloved friend, Mary Cipriani-Price, I love helping hurting hearts with you. You created a safe space for me to share my pain. God used you to start the path to writing this book. Thank you for listening, caring, and challenging me on my healing journey. I am so glad God blessed me with you.

To my pastor, Bishop A. B. Vines, and the New Seasons Church family, thank you for reminding me I am fearfully and wonderfully made, blessed to be a blessing, and the apple of God's eye. Your prayers, support, love, and encouragement continue to bless me.

To my agent, Dr. Sharon Norris Elliott, I thank God for creating our divine appointment. Thank you for guiding, inspiring, believing, and supporting me during my writing journey. I am incredibly grateful you accepted me as your client. We did it!

To my book coach, Christine Gail, you taught me so much. You encouraged, challenged, cajoled, and tugged this book into existence. You had faith in me when I did not have it in myself.

Thank you to the Elk Lake Publishing family—Deb, Susan, and Judy, who accepted the idea for this book and patiently worked with me during my difficult season of my mother going home to be with the Lord.

A special thanks to Carrie for her editorial help, spiritual insight, and ongoing support in bringing *Tapestry* to life. Thank you for correcting my manuscript with compassionate care.

To my Heavenly Father. To my Lord and Savior, Jesus Christ. To Holy Spirit, the true Author of this book. My eyes are filled with tears of joy as I reflect on our journey together. I do not have the words to convey my love and gratitude to You. To God be all the glory, Amen.

MY HEART FOR YOU

Before we begin, I want to acknowledge your courage in picking up this book at all and to offer a word of caution. Take your time reading this book. If you feel overwhelmed, put the book down for a short time. During the first counseling session, I explain the healing process to my clients. Therapy usually gets ugly before it gets beautiful. If you have ever broken a bone, you know exactly what I mean.

I went to an orthopedic doctor three weeks after I broke the tip of my index finger. The doctor grasped my damaged digit and began to bend it. Tears streamed down my face as I tried to yank my hand back. I never wanted to hit a woman so badly in my life. Finally, she let go and offered me a tissue. "I'm sorry I had to do that to you, but your finger had started to heal incorrectly. If I didn't bend it, you would never be able to make a fist again." Following weeks of physical therapy, all my fingers curl now as they should, and my fist can be ready for use at any time.

Traveling through the pain to get to healing is difficult. Praise God, he promises to journey with us. "Even when I walk through the darkest valley, I will not be afraid, for you are close beside me" (Psalm 23:4). Notice the psalmist said, "through the valley," not around, over, or under. You must go through, but you don't have to go alone. My sister,

I wish I could sit beside you, to encourage and support you. Since I cannot, I urge you to find someone for support and comfort and to give you feedback. Choose your spouse, a trustworthy friend, a close family member, or a therapist.

Although I am a marriage and family therapist, this book is not intended to provide mental health or relationship treatment. My goal is to educate and provide information as self-help tool for your own use. The information in this book is meant to supplement, not replace, the benefits of a therapeutic professional relationship. Please read "Signs It's Time to Seek a Therapist" in the Resource section.

If the content of this book stirs up painful memories or sparks a reaction in your body, give yourself an emotional break—set the book aside, seek the comfort of your loved one, and ask God for strength to continue. Don't be surprised by the powerful emotions you may experience. Give yourself permission to feel the feelings. But not alone. Seek support. "Two people are better off than one, for they can help each other succeed. If one person falls, the other can reach out and help. But someone who falls alone is in real trouble." (Ecclesiastes 4:9–10) When you are calm again, I urge you to press on through this book to reach for the healing threads God has for waiting for you.

Okay, now take a deep breath, hold, and release. Ready to keep reading? Let's go.

PART I:
WOUNDED BY CHILDHOOD SEXUAL ABUSE

—CHAPTER 1—
A NEW VIEW: DISCOVER GOD'S PERSPECTIVE

"That's why we can be so sure that every detail in our lives of love for God is worked into something good."
Romans 8:28 MSG

"There is healing for every seemingly unhealable scar. Comfort for the feelings of, 'I've gone too far.' Identity for the moments when we've forgotten who we are in his arms."

Morgan Harper-Nichols

Tears sprang to my eyes. I was stunned. My friend was stunned. Neither of us was prepared for the moment that would change the rest of my life. My friend Mary and I are marriage and family therapists, which is a fancy way of saying we are counselors who help people with hurting hearts. We had a break between counseling sessions, and we were catching up on events in our lives when the conversation turned to the weight issues with which we both struggled. We lamented how discouraging it was to help other people but remain unsuccessful in our own lives.

I cannot remember the exact question she asked which caused my heartbeat to suddenly race. I do distinctly remember, though, feeling threatened and wanting to run, but my body was glued to my chair. Words flew out of my mouth before I could grab them and bring them back.

"If I lose weight, men will notice me and hurt me," I exclaimed.

I honestly had no idea where those words came from, but they defined a clear, foundational truth I believed and lived—a truth that, up until that moment, I had never realized guided my whole life. These words unlocked a secret I had never shared with her before. How could I have shared it? Like I said, that secret had just crystalized for me.

We had been friends since our days as interns studying to become therapists, over twenty-five years, and yet I had never shared the hurt of my past with her before. I had kept it so deeply buried, hidden from my own self, I had literally forgotten about it.

But it never forgot about me.

I looked at Mary as the truth came into sharp focus in my brain. The weight was secondary. I had wrapped the weight around myself as a protective camouflage. Then more painful words tumbled out.

"I was molested as a child."

The lid I had secured so tightly on my secret had been loosened, and everything I had held in for so long—every emotion, every pain—came gushing out. My wide-eyed friend opened her mouth to speak, but the bell indicating that my next client had arrived abruptly ended our conversation.

I quickly stuffed everything back deep down and slammed the lid shut, but to my horror the lid didn't fit as tightly anymore. Oh, the agony of that moment. I may have been released from that painful conversation in the moment, but I knew I would soon have to deal with my feelings on a deeper level. I had no choice. So, I pushed my own needs down and took care of my client. This was no time to display my own issues.

Later that night, Mary emailed to say she was sorry I had such pain and asked why I had never told her about it before. I didn't really have an answer. I really had no idea the trauma of my past had been wreaking such havoc on my present. Here I was, the person trained to help other people with their trauma, yet I had not dealt with my own. Instead, I had repeatedly buried the memory of my trauma and forgotten its existence.

The first time I used this self-defense tool occurred after I told my mother about my abuse. Years later, sex education lessons triggered my abuse memories, and I thought I was pregnant. Terrified, I shared my fear with my mom, believing this was my first disclosure. She comforted me. "Baby, you told me about the abuse. Don't you remember? We stopped contact with your abuser to protect you. And you are not pregnant!" To this day, I do not remember telling her my secret. Throughout my life this pattern continued. Memories of the abuse surfaced, but I sent them deep into the crevices of my mind as if it never happened. After telling Mary, my truth refused to hide.

My coping skills had trapped me in the tangles of my past. Wrapped in isolation, struggling with guilt and shame, I sought relief in all the wrong places. My desperation led me to God. He helped me navigate the blame, shame, staggering guilt, lost hope, dark depression, and vast emptiness I experienced following my abuse. He led me to Scriptures and biblical accounts to comfort, guide, and heal my heart. God knew the time was right to handle this business, and I'm glad he got the ball rolling. He started me on a journey of healing that has been tough yet amazing. Now I get to share my journey with you.

Hopefully, you picked up this book before having an earth-shattering moment like the one I had in my friend's office. Or maybe you have come to a point in your life where you realize your past is controlling your present, and if you don't do something quick, it will most likely control your future as well. Maybe you have just decided enough is enough—it is time to live the life God wants you to have. The trauma of childhood sexual abuse has dominated your life long enough, and now it is time to claim the healing God offers each of us.

WE ARE NOT ALONE

Almost daily I encounter women who struggle with the trauma of their past childhood sexual abuse. Whether they are clients, friends, or family members, I hear and understand their struggles as women share their pain with me. The damage caused by sexual abuse does not discriminate. It ravages all cultures, all ages, and all backgrounds as evidence of its existence is splashed across the media.

The #MeToo movement grew in numbers daily as many women came forward to admit they were sexually abused. Then the #WeToo movement sprang up, identifying sexual abuse victims in the church. Thousands of women who had been silenced by shame and fear of rejection were emboldened to step forward in massive numbers.

According to the Rape, Abuse, and Incest National Network (RAINN), every 92 seconds an American is sexually assaulted, and every nine minutes that victim is a child. My heart breaks for every one of them. RAINN also reports 82 percent of all victims under 18 are female.[1]

Dr. Larry Nasser, the former professor at Michigan State University and USA Gymnastics national team doctor, is in prison serving a sentence of 40–175 years for molesting his young patients over a period of more than two decades. Over 160 of the 265 victimized women came forward to speak at his sentencing.[2]

You may be able to relate to some of those courageous ladies. I know I can. Do any of these words, thoughts, or feelings sound familiar?

Speaking of times when she tried to reveal what was happening to her, gymnast Katie Rasmussen said, "No one did anything because no one believed me. They didn't understand how such a respectable doctor would do something like that. And I don't understand how a fourteen-year-old could make that up."[3]

Physical therapist and former gymnast Marta Stern said she originally wanted to remain anonymous "out of fear of how it would affect [her] life, loved ones, and career."[4]

Every one of us has a different story to tell. We may not have been abused by our doctor, but in the majority of our cases, we were victimized by someone we should have been able to trust like a parent, a priest, a teacher, a coach, or a babysitter. You may have tried to tell someone about your abuse, but you weren't believed. Perhaps you were told you misunderstood, made it up, or were trying to get someone in trouble. Some of you may have kept silent because you were afraid. If people knew what happened to you, they would look at you differently, and your life could change for the worse.

Many of us want to lock the experience of our abuse in a dungeon, hoping it will never again see the light of day. Life goes on, but then something triggers the pain. The dungeon opens and the trauma caused by the abuse comes roaring to life until we can grab it to force it back in the cell again. In those moments when the pain erupts, we feel as though the perpetrator took both our innocence and our control in life. Healing, wholeness, and power seem lost forever.

As I've listened to one painful story after another, I've come to realize there are common threads woven into those painful tales. In our pain, we tend to focus on the dark damage caused by the trauma, shame, discouragement, and fear. We see the tangled mess of our lives with little hope for healing. The ability to tamp down our self-preservation instincts and learn to trust others, including God, can feel beyond our reach.

But there is good news. God wants to heal us from past abuse so it cannot define our future. He wants us to exchange our narrow focus on the pain for his expansive view. Like a master weaver, he sees the broader picture of light and healing created through commitment, perseverance, hope, faith, and forgiveness. I deeply desire to share my story of healing and show you how transformation of the past is possible when we see ourselves through our Heavenly Father's eyes.

One Bible account captured my attention and inspired me to pursue my own healing. I learned about a woman who suffered physically for twelve years but never gave up hope. Finally, after trying everything else, she turned to Jesus and her hope for healing became reality. Curious, I dove deeper into the verses describing her journey. I discovered qualities, practical applications, and essential tools which I applied to my own life—truths that transformed my trauma to triumph and exchanged my life as a victim into the life of a victorious and vibrant human being.

Take a Breath

I congratulate you for making it through this first chapter. Some of that information was difficult and may have stirred up some painful memories. If that is true for you, I encourage you to take a rest before continuing to the next chapter. God won't penalize you and neither will I! Give yourself permission to proceed at your own pace.

God wants to heal you and give you abundant life, so I will end each chapter with some practical activities to help you understand your tapestry. First, the Tapestry Truths will boil down the main points of the chapter into simple, easy-to-remember statements. Next the Tapestry Tips will invite you to take physical steps on your healing journey. Take my hand, my sister, and let's continue together.

Tapestry Truths

- You are not alone.
- We each have a unique story, but we are in this together.
- God has a plan for your healing.

Tapestry Tips

One of the most effective healing tools is journaling. For some people this comes very naturally. For others, like me, not so much, so writing prompts can be helpful. Feel free to use the blank lines below or treat yourself to a new journal in which you can record your healing journey. Think of your journaling as an opportunity to pour out your heart to God. Here is your first prompt:

1. What feelings surfaced as you read this chapter?

2. Write yourself a note of congratulations for having made it this far. Be sure to include some encouragement to continue the journey and reach for God's healing.

—CHAPTER 2—
OUR TAPESTRY: UNTANGLE THE THREADS

I want you woven into a tapestry of love, in touch with everything there is to know of God. Then you will have minds confident and at rest, focused on Christ, God's great mystery.

Colossians 2:2 MSG

"God is able to thread together the good, the bad, and the bitter experiences life has taken us through to shape a beautiful masterpiece of destiny and accomplish his purpose in our lives."
Dr. Tony Evans, *Detours: The Unpredictable Path to Your Destiny*.

TAPESTRY

When I review painful episodes that stole my childhood and my innocence, of course I wish they had not occurred. I struggle to understand how God could have let them happen. Even more difficult is imagining how God can make something beautiful out of the ugly mess left behind. But let's reread the verse above.

I want you woven into a tapestry of love, in touch with everything there is to know of God. Then you will have minds confident and at rest, focused on Christ, God's great mystery. (Colossians 2:2 MSG)

This verse encourages believers to become part of God's tapestry of love by learning about him and his heart for you. When your focus shifts away from your pain and struggles, and instead turns to Christ, you receive two benefits—confidence and rest. Isn't that what we long for? Our minds don't need to be controlled by our past because they can be filled with hope and healing when we focus on Christ.

God has custom designed each of our lives to be a tapestry that tells his story of love. "For we are God's masterpiece. He has created us anew in Christ Jesus, so we can do the good things he planned for us long ago" (Ephesians 2:10). Merriam-Webster defines masterpiece as "a work done with extraordinary skill" and emphasizes it especially refers to "a supreme intellectual or artistic achievement." As God's masterpiece, we are the work done with extraordinary skill. We become his artistic achievement.

None of us feel like a masterpiece when the pain of our abuse colors our view of self. While we tend to see ourselves through the lens of abuse survivors, abuse and the resulting effects are only part of our identity, not the whole. If we will take the difficult steps to turn our focus on Christ, he will produce a beautiful tapestry from our trauma.

Tapestries are works of art depicting religious scenes or historical events, but they also served a purpose. Historically, the woven fabric was a practical means to block drafts of cold air. Additionally, the decorative works added color while conveying spiritual and expressive messages to viewers. "They [tapestries] remain a powerful reminder that in today's sea of social media, if you ever find yourself at a loss for words, you can still say it with a tapestry."[1] Tapestries provided entertainment and food for thought thanks to the vibrant messages displayed on these exquisite works of art.

The process of making a tapestry is complicated, especially for someone like me who is not crafty or naturally artistic. By definition, "a tapestry is a weft-faced plain weave with discontinuous wefts that conceal all its warps. Simply weave the warp and weft threads together, and voilà—you have a tapestry!"[2] You're probably asking, "What is this woman talking about?"

A tapestry is made when vertical (warp) threads are fixed on a large frame (loom) and horizontal (weft) threads are woven through. When the weft threads are squished (tamped) down very close together, the warp threads are completely hidden.

WARP: We Are Reliving Pain

The vertical warp threads are vital components because, when fixed to the top and bottom of the loom, they are the foundation for the tapestry. I compare the negative effects of childhood sexual abuse to these warp threads. When we were abused, dark threads were fixed to the loom of our lives and create our tapestry foundation. As survivors we tend to focus on the dark warp threads causing us to relive the painful experiences.

WEFT: We Experience Full Transformation

After the warps are attached to the loom, the weaver covers them with the bright colors of the horizontal weft threads. I compare God's healing work to these weft threads. From left to right and back again, the beautiful wefts are woven over and under the warps to form the picture we see on the tapestry. The wefts are squeezed tightly together, and although the warps are present, they are no longer the focus. How powerful! The pain of the dark warp threads becomes invisible as God weaves in the healing weft threads to form our tapestry.

My sister, I want to prepare you. The next five chapters will identify five warp threads tied to our looms by the abuse we suffered. First, we will define trauma, triggers, shame, discouragement, and fear. Then we will discuss the impact of these dark threads in our lives and some practical steps for dealing with those effects. I know these will be difficult chapters to read, so I encourage to you to read them slowly, take breaks when you need them, and seek the support of loved ones. Most importantly, lean into our mighty God for strength and motivation to press on.

The wonderful news is that after we identify the dark warp threads, we will focus on the bright weft threads. As we discuss commitment, perseverance, hope, faith, and forgiveness, God's masterpiece will begin to take shape and he will reveal beautiful healing in our lives. If you become overwhelmed reading about the warp threads, please take an emotional break—but don't give up entirely. My sister, the practical action steps in the later chapters will encourage your wounded heart and allow God to apply those beautiful, cheerful colors to the masterpiece tapestry he wants to make of you.

TAPESTRY TRUTHS

- Warp threads have laid a dark foundation in our lives.
- Bright weft threads can cover that darkness.
- God is the master weaver who uses all those threads to create a beautiful tapestry of our lives.

TAPESTRY TIPS

1. Write out a prayer telling God what you think your tapestry might look like right now and what you'd like it to look like when he is finished.

—CHAPTER 3—
THE RED THREAD OF TRAUMA:
ACKNOWLEDGE THE DAMAGE

"The LORD is close to the brokenhearted; he rescues those whose spirits are crushed."
Psalm 34:18

Everything is both simpler than we can imagine and more entangled than we can conceive.
—Johann Wolfgang von Goethe

Years ago, while shopping, I encountered a lady who knew me as a child. We chatted about people we knew and enjoyed a delightful conversation ... until she inquired about him. Shocked, I battled to maintain a pleasant smile while my insides quivered and screamed *"Run!"* Instantly, I transformed from confident professional woman into a frightened little girl. I babbled an excuse and bolted. My eyes darted back and forth, terrified I might see my perpetrator. My heart beat a rapid rhythm as I sought safety. I escaped her questions but not the reaction to my past. Unknowingly, I became entangled by the red thread of my childhood trauma.

Red is generally used to depict the devil, anger, and shame, as illustrated by the *Scarlet Letter*. The damage inflicted by our perpetrators at a tender age stained our hearts, minds, and bodies. My physical and emotional reaction to hearing my perpetrator's name—even decades later while in a safe, public space—is common for abuse victims. Maybe you've experienced something similar. What is it about trauma that makes our bodies respond this way?

What Is Trauma?

Trauma has become a buzz word we hear tossed around a lot—in the news, in our living rooms, on the Dr. Phil show. But what does this word truly mean? Why does this six-letter word have such a huge impact on our lives?

Trauma is commonly defined as "exposure to actual or threatened death, serious injury, or sexual violation in which intense fear, horror, or helplessness predominates. This can occur either through one single event or multiple and repeated traumatic events."[1]

Say what? Let me make it real. Trauma begins with the act of something serious happening to you. That something could be watching someone die, someone threatening to kill you, or even a serious injury in a car accident. The act that presently concerns us, however, is sexual violation as a child. This can range from being photographed for the abuser's pleasure to seeing explicit photographs to molestation, rape, and a whole lot of variations in between. The depth of the impact trauma has on us is determined by our reaction to the event or situation. Dr. Gabor Maté explains, "Trauma is not what happens to you. Trauma is what happens inside you as a result of what happens to you."[2]

Professor Christiane Sanderson explains complex trauma is usually associated with prolonged, repeated traumatic experiences involving multiple violations such as sexual assaults, physical violence, emotional abuse, and neglect, often committed by someone known to the victim.

Unlike a single traumatic event, Sanderson says that when the betrayal of trust is repeated and 'the abuse masquerades as protection or affection,' a range of symptoms can appear, "such as dissociation, alterations in sense of self, and a fear of intimacy in relationships."[3]

There is something excruciating and complicated when someone entrusted to protect you is the one you need protection from. In my case, my parents trusted a close friend of the family, never knowing I was hurt on each visit. And as good, responsible parents, they reminded me, "Do what he tells you to do. Respect your elders." Unknowingly, they set me up for a predator. *I am supposed to trust you, but you are the one hurting me. Why are my parents telling me to obey you?*

Talk about complicated. Honestly, on another level, I felt betrayed not only by the man who hurt me but also by my parents. They didn't have a clue what was happening to me, and because of their ignorance, they failed to protect me. Please don't get me wrong, I do not blame them at all. My head understood they believed I was safe and protected, but my heart didn't agree.

Complex. Complicated. Confusing. Messy. Tangled. Is it any wonder healing from childhood sexual abuse doesn't happen immediately or overnight? A child can be abused repeatedly for days, weeks, months, and sometimes years. As the abuse happens over time, so the skills needed to survive develop over time. Likewise, time is needed to grow healthier coping skills and heal a broken heart. My heart aches for you, my co-sufferers. I can't begin to imagine your traumatic experiences, but I know our God can untangle, clean, clarify, and simplify as he works on the artistry of our lives.

As adult survivors of childhood sexual abuse, there may be signs or evidence of the impact of abuse on our lives today. Until those words escaped my mouth, I had no idea my life was controlled by the red thread of trauma. I wanted to remain invisible to men, and I chose food to avoid the pain. I lived my life believing I needed to protect myself from a threat that no longer existed. However, recognition of the negative impact of my symptoms started my journey toward my healing.

As survivors of childhood sexual abuse, we have experiences as adults, which we may not recognize as related to the trauma. No two stories are alike. Each of our ordeals is unique, but there are commonalties. Seemingly normal situations make cause us stress or fear. Healthy relationships might feel out of reach. Even our physical health can suffer. When you have support nearby and are feeling prepared, look at the list in appendix A. Do you recognize some of the effects on your adult life? The list isn't meant to be a diagnosis, but rather to help you recognize the source of your adult difficulties. Just as I did when I blurted out why I didn't lose weight.

God's heart breaks to see his children still experiencing the coping tools we used to protect ourselves during the abuse and guard against overwhelming feelings of helplessness and terror. Although some coping strategies may eventually lead to health problems, they helped us make it to adulthood. When these tools become worn out and ineffective, we may feel even more guilt because we didn't recognize the problems and do something about them earlier. I know I felt the same way. But we're no longer the helpless child. I pray your perpetrator is no longer able to hurt you physically. They did not win. Your coping skills did the job, and you are alive.

While we did survive, the sexual abuse undoubtedly took a toll on our relationships. The list of symptoms in appendix A shows the responses to abuse can be extreme.

One survivor may believe her life has little to no meaning without a partner, so she focuses on her partner's needs while ignoring her own. Another survivor may avoid relationships so no one will have the power to hurt her. These same actions may be meted out to family members or friends as well. Either the survivor takes care of everyone except herself or refuses to get too close to anyone. This lack of trust may also inhibit secure, healthy physical intimacy. You see, trust is the primary issue in relationships. The cry from the wounded heart laments, "How can I trust you not to hurt or betray me?"

Childhood sexual abuse has the power to deprive us of something we desperately need. In our struggle to protect ourselves from re-injury, we shy away from the comfort of connection. My desire is for you to begin to take the necessary steps which will lead you to the power of a healthy relationship. The red warp thread of trauma threatens to keep us entangled and isolated. God has a better plan.

God designed us for connection, and the Trinity models this design for us. God the Father, God the Son, and God the Holy Spirit are never out of sync. When he created Adam, the first man, he said it was not good for man to be alone. God performed the first surgery, removing Adam's rib to fashion Eve, and the two became the first couple of all humanity. Proverbs 27:9 (MSG) tells us "A sweet friendship refreshes the soul." We are created for relationship.

During the process of creating a tapestry, the weaver works facing the back of the tapestry. But in front of the tapestry, he places a mirror to see the forming artwork through the warp threads. While working on the complicated messy back, he sees the emerging beauty of the tapestry in the making.

God is our weaver. While we stay focused on the mess of our lives, he looks through the dark warp threads and sees the beauty the weft threads are creating. God sees the full picture. I long for you to also see through the warps into the mirror of God's word and recognize the masterpiece he is creating of your life.

We can choose vibrant wefts designed to promote hope and healing on the loom of our life. We can choose the wefts to hand to God so he can create the masterpiece he desires of our lives. In later chapters of this book, we will explore the colorful wefts which represent tangible skills necessary for healing from child abuse trauma.

I like the way God says he reaches out to us "to provide for those who mourn in Zion; to give them a crown of beauty instead of ashes, festive oil instead of mourning, and splendid clothes instead of despair" (Isaiah 61:3 HCSB). From the ashes of our childhood trauma, God longs to give us a crown of beauty to transform our grief into joy and to cover the dark warp threads of our lives with radiant weft treads to create beautiful artistry.

The words of Paul's prayer for his friends are my prayer for you. "I want you woven into a tapestry of love, in touch with everything there is to know of God. Then you will have minds confident and at rest, focused on Christ, God's great mystery" (Colossians 2:2 MSG).

Now is the time to develop healthier coping skills. It is time to make sense of the tangles of childhood sexual abuse and allow God to transform them into a masterpiece. It's now our turn to take back the control of our lives from the devastating memories of abuse and begin weaving meaningful, valuable relationships with God and others. Allow God's unconditional love and hope to penetrate your heart.

TAPESTRY TRUTHS

- The red thread of trauma symbolizes the damage caused by childhood sexual abuse.
- The coping skills you developed were ways to protect yourself, but they may deny you the pleasure of a healthy relationship.
- It is time to make sense of the tangles of childhood sexual abuse and transform them into God's masterpiece.

TAPESTRY TIPS

1. Identifying personal aspects of our painful story of childhood sexual abuse may be a struggle, and I understand. As part of the healing process, it is helpful to recognize any problems and how they may affect us. Pray and seek God's guidance before tackling this exercise. If the answer is, "not yet," Move to the next chapter with my blessings. If you choose to continue, please use your support system. Also, have a pleasurable activity planned as a reward and self-care after you finish.

2. Review the list of effects of childhood sexual abuse in Appendix A. Circle the symptoms that apply to you. Check the statements below that apply to your story.

    ☐ I did not recall any sexual abuse in my past until a memory came back out of nowhere.

    ☐ I feel fine about my body.

    ☐ I feel shame because of the abuse.

    ☐ I know he or she abused me, but I feel like I'm to blame.

- ☐ I feel alone and misunderstood.
- ☐ I believe if people knew my story, they would not love me.
- ☐ I feel like my body betrayed me.
- ☐ I attempt to numb my pain by over- or under-eating, substance abuse, or self-mutilation.
- ☐ Sometimes I still think I made it all up.

3. Read Psalm 31:9 & 22

   Have mercy on me, Lord, for I am in distress.
   Tears blur my eyes.
   My body and soul are withering away.
   In panic I cried out,
   "I am cut off from the Lord!"
   But you heard my cry for mercy
   and answered my call for help."

4. What is God saying to you today through this verse? What does the verse say God will do? Share your pain with God and ask him to help you.

—CHAPTER 4—
THE BROWN THREAD OF TRIGGERS: UNDERSTAND THE SURVIVAL SKILLS

> But the Lord is faithful; He will strengthen and guard you from the evil one.
> 2 Thessalonians 3:3 HCSB

> We aren't the weeds in the crack of life. We're the strong, amazing flowers that found a way to grow in the most challenging conditions.
> —Jeanne McElvaney

I imagine you experienced difficulty reading the previous chapter regarding the symptoms of childhood sexual abuse. Hold on, my sister—time to go a little deeper. Many want to leave the pain of childhood sexual abuse in the past. After all, we are no longer children. The people who hurt us don't have power over our lives or bodies any longer. However, our past pain remains our present reality.

As I said earlier, I thought my life was fine until that moment in my friend's office. I was not fine. I was tangled. My painful history was not past—it was present. The moment my friend said something about losing weight, I panicked. Instantly, the idea of becoming visible and noticed by men brought an unconscious sense of danger to mind. Feelings of dread, desperation, despair, and terror flooded my soul. My mind perceived immediate jeopardy and reacted by transporting me back in time to my abuse. My mind had recognized a threat and gone into protect mode.

The sound of my office doorbell brought me back to the present, but I was shaken. Breathing deeply, I pulled myself together, buried my pain, and continued work. The brown warp thread of triggers yanked tightly in the recess of my subconscious as I relived pain.

A trigger is something that mentally sends you back in time to the event of your trauma and causes an emotional response seemingly out of proportion to the current circumstances. I remember a time when my husband pulled into a parking spot and bumped the curb. Immediately my mind flashed back to a previous car accident. My heart raced, my breathing increased, and my body braced for impact. There was no danger, but my mind reacted to the *threat* of danger.

The brown thread of triggers bogs us down like mud and leaves us feeling dirty and defeated. Repeatedly controlled by our past, we wonder if we will ever be free or feel clean in the future.

What Are Triggers?

God created our brains to make survival the top priority. Anyone, anything, any situation perceived as a danger signals our central nervous system to automatically go into protect mode. We don't have to think about it.

Within the central nervous system, the sympathetic nervous system sounds an alarm to mobilize either fight or flight. The parasympathetic nervous system, on the other hand, is a red light to freeze—to conserve energy by not moving. Think of it this way. The sympathetic nervous system says, "Don't just stand there, do something," while the parasympathetic nervous system says, "Don't do anything, just stand there!" I'll talk about the parasympathetic nervous system in more detail in the next chapter.

Triggers activate our sympathetic nervous system as a call-to-action button. Our bodies react to threatening events, but also respond to the possibility of something bad happening. Did you catch that? Our bodies respond to the possibility of a threat, not necessarily to the reality of an actual threat, including danger signals experienced previously. Like déjà vu, our bodies say, "Been here, done this."

These sparks of memory can range from devastating to mild, some almost indiscernible to the abuse survivor. The brain recognizes danger via one of the five senses—sight, sound, touch, taste, or smell—and triggers an emergency message to the body. One client became nauseous when she smelled her perpetrator's favorite flavor of gum. If your perpetrator had a beard, you may find yourself uncomfortable around men with beards. Triggers come in many forms. Underline or circle the triggers below that you've experienced.

TRIGGER TYPES

- People: physical traits, like baldness or a certain body type
- Time: times of day, days of the week, times of year, anniversary dates
- Colors: specifically colored items, like blue walls or red shirts
- Things: particular objects, like a quilt or a lampshade
- Places: the scene or neighborhood of abuse or similar locations, like a beach or park.
- Entertainment: TV, news, books, or social media showing or describing a trauma similar to yours

- Smell: Certain colognes or perfumes
- Sounds: noises, songs, or voices
- Taste: foods or drinks
- Words: reading or hearing certain words or phrases
- Touch: a touch on a certain body part in a way like your abuse
- Situations: someone hugging you from behind suddenly
- Feelings: emotions experienced during abuse like fear, helplessness, pain, or stress

In childhood, our brains warned us of the threat of abuse and sent our bodies into protect mode. Unfortunately, our brains missed the memo that said, "Perpetrator gone, episodes of abuse terminated." Now that brown warp thread of triggers entangles us. When our bodies recognize a reminder of a threat, we experience those same feelings, sensations, and impulses as when the danger was real.

In common situations, emotions resolve spontaneously. For example, when we watch a scary movie, we jump when the villain explodes on the scene to create havoc. Eventually the adrenaline subsides, and we relax and enjoy the rest of the movie. But triggers elicit sudden, intense feelings that grip tightly and won't let go. I hate horror movies. They are a trigger for me that creates a longer recovery time, leaving me shaken and helpless.

My first counseling job as a therapist intern was at the only child abuse clinic in all of San Diego. I learned a lot about childhood sexual abuse working at the clinic and trying to help children and their families heal from abuse. I also had the privilege to work with adults who were molested as children. Some of them knew their history, but others, like me, did not.

During a session early in my career, a woman struggled to understand her fear of her husband bathing their infant daughter. My client, let's call her Trisha, was a new mom of a baby girl who feared her husband might hurt her daughter. Her fear was so pronounced that she prevented her husband from having time alone with the baby. Her lack of trust created a wedge between the two of them, and she no longer wanted to be physically intimate with him. She was perplexed because, prior to giving birth, they had a great marriage. There was no history of abuse, nothing tangible to feed her fear. Her whole family was distressed and confused.

During our sessions, we talked about the times she felt protective and afraid. Then we explored her childhood. Stunned, her eyes filled with tears as a painful memory surfaced. "I was molested! Oh, my goodness. I never remembered that before." Someone she loved and trusted had betrayed and abused her. She feared her husband, whom she loved and trusted, would betray their daughter in the same way even though there was no real threat to her daughter. Her brain reacted, and her past pain impacted her present relationship.

Trauma affects us in many ways, so I always use the final session with parents of sexually abused children to share potential future triggers. I explain trauma symptoms may return for a bit during specific seasons of their daughter's life, such as when she begins her menstrual cycle, when she starts dating or begins sexual activity, or when she gives birth to a daughter. The new mom's instinctive desire to protect her child from danger may trigger negative responses which impact her relationship with her partner. Fears from the past can cause her to push him away because she cannot trust him not to hurt her daughter. I repeat, these are potential triggers which may or may not occur.

Some of you may be able to relate while others may not. Trisha recognized the possibility of danger to her daughter and knew to protect her without understanding why she felt inordinately strong about this. But she put her husband in the role of the perpetrator even though he was innocent. Trisha unknowingly risked damaging her marriage in her desire to keep her daughter safe. She had the right motivation but the wrong execution.

Here's the tricky part. My client's past also impacted my present. In the middle of her revelation, memories of my own molestation came barreling through my brain with the power of a locomotive. Although I worked with abuse victims for months, my molestation memories had not surfaced. During the interview process for my internship, my supervisor asked if I experienced childhood sexual abuse. I replied no. I did not realize I had buried the pain of my trauma so deeply, which is why I thought I answered honestly. Like my sixth-grade sex education lessons, Trisha's narrative opened my memory vault and released the horror of my own abuse story. Like a flash flood, agonizing images washed over me as I relived my painful past anew.

Horrible timing, right? I had to help my client with her pain while pushing my own nightmare back down in the recesses of my mind. I needed the promise of Christ's strength, "I can do all things through Christ who strengthens me" (Philippians 4:13 NKJV). Christ equipped me to serve her amid my pain. Trisha's story of her betrayal pain resonated deep in own my soul. I had worked for months helping other survivors with their traumatic histories. Now here I was, face to face with my abuse as my heart whispered, "Me too." But as Trisha left my office, my defenses kicked in once again to stuff down that memory and protect me from the pain. The trigger would trip again so many years later in Mary's office, but I was safe for the moment.

Can you relate? You find yourself living your customary life, then suddenly Blam! Your life no longer feels safe. Instead, life feels doomed. Or perhaps your reactions don't make sense or match the situation, like experiencing overwhelming fear that your loving, gentle husband will hurt your daughter. Triggers that once protected are now outdated and create damage.

FLASHBACKS

Flashbacks, nightmares, panic attacks, or disassociation (emotionally or mentally withdrawing) are particularly distressing triggers because they seem to occur without warning. We feel as though we don't have control over our minds and bodies, like how we had no control over our abuse. The truth is we do have control in these instances. We may suffer from these symptoms, but our healing journey includes learning how to manage them.

Flashbacks take us back to our trauma with vivid Technicolor and surround sound. Our bodies are in the present, but our minds are in the past as we reexperience our abuse. While a flashback is only a memory, the experience is so powerful our bodies produce the same hormones we needed during our past trauma. we are no longer the little girl desperate to escape the perpetrator, but our bodies are trying to defend against the danger of past trauma.

A nightmare is a flashback which occurs while asleep. Any symptoms we may experience are normal as our subconscious takes us back to our trauma. Helplessly, we are held captive by our dreams as we relive painful events until we finally wake up in our own beds. We may wake up drenched in sweat with a heart racing in fear. Sister, you are not crazy. Even though it may feel like it, you are not losing your mind. No wonder many suffer from insomnia. At the end of this chapter, I suggest some exercises which may help you with your struggles.

Dissociation refers to emotionally or mentally withdrawing from the traumatic situation to draw less attention to a threat. I'm trying not to be too technical here. I call it mentally checking out. Our bodies are physically present, but our minds pull deep inside and shut down. Have you ever experienced driving home, but you don't remember how you arrived in your driveway? That is a form of dissociation. A portion of you drove automatically, but the thinking and feeling part was focused somewhere else completely.

GOD'S SAFETY PLAN

I imagine you are wondering how the brown warp thread of triggers helped you survive your childhood sexual abuse, especially since those triggers now have your sense of safety and wellbeing in a tangle. Think for a moment about your past trauma, which likely occurred multiple times. Your nervous system sounded the alarm to warn you and to send your body into protect mode. I can hear your protests now. "But, Donna, it didn't work. I was still hurt!" Correct, you were injured despite your brain and body doing its best to defend you. My heart hurts with you. I cannot begin to imagine your pain, the horror, and the helplessness. But while your child-sized body could not physically protect you from a threat bigger than yourself (your perpetrator), your nervous system did protect you in other ways. If you disassociated, for example, your emotional and mental withdrawal prevented you from fully experiencing the trauma. The sound of slurred speech, the smell of certain cologne, or the sight of a particular room signaled danger, and you knew it was time to mentally hide.

So now that we are not children anymore and our perpetrators no longer hurt us, how do we stop our defective internal defense system that continues to warn us of danger? We turn to God and allow Him to direct us in our fight against triggers. "But the Lord is faithful; He will strengthen and guard you from the evil one" (2 Thessalonians 3:3 HCSB). This verse reminds us that we are fighting against the devil. When he wants to push us away from our loving God, he sends a reminder of our past trauma to kick us into survival mode.

Let's replace our old, outdated defense system with an eternally effective upgrade called the Armor of God found in Ephesians 6:14-18. The apostle Paul provided a list of protective gear and weapons to defend against enemy fire and go on the attack. By strengthening our relationship with God, we beat back the effects of our trauma, neutralize the threat of our triggers, and tell our central nervous system to stand down. Appendix B studies each piece of God's armor and how we can use them to win the battle in our hearts and minds.

Recovering from childhood sexual abuse takes time. The healing process is painful. With prayer and practice, you can regain your sense of control, rebuild your self-worth, and learn to heal.

TAPESTRY TRUTHS

- The brown thread of triggers may entangle you now, but they enabled you to survive then.
- Flashbacks are just another way your brain is trying to protect you from danger.
- Replace your old, outdated defense system with an eternally effective upgrade called the Armor of God (see Armor of God in Appendix B).

TAPESTRY TIPS

1. Read Appendix B before proceeding to the next chapter. Identify one piece of God's armor you will don as part of your new defense against triggers.

2. In your journal, jot down any triggers which may have caused a flashback. Next, think of various ways you may remind yourself, "This is a flashback," and stay in the present. For example, deep breathing or twisting a ring on your finger. Write down a statement you can repeat aloud like, "This is a memory, not the trauma. I am safe. I am okay." You may want to use a verse as your mantra. One of my favorites is "I will be with you when you pass through the waters, and when you pass through the rivers, they will not overwhelm you. You will not be scorched when you walk through the fire, and the flame will not burn you" (Isaiah 43:2 HCSB).

2. Grounding is a way to distract you from flashback and help you refocus on what's happening in the moment. One of my clients looks around for her favorite color which helps her feel grounded in the moment. My favorite one is 5-4-3-2-1.

- Breathe deeply and place your feet flat on the ground.
- Identify five things you can see around you. It could be this book, a blanket, the wall, or a water bottle.
- Identify and touch four things you can feel. Your clothes, your hair, jewelry, or a pillow.
- Identify three things you can hear as you listen—traffic, music, or voices.
- Identify two things you can smell, like a scented candle, air freshener, or perfume.
- Identify one thing you can taste in your mouth. Gum, toothpaste, or coffee lingering on your tongue.

Grounding techniques come with many options. Commit to practice daily during non-stressful times. Build up to two or three times per day. Consistency will equip your mind and body to react to the flashback in a healthier way. Do some research to find a technique that works best for you and write it down here.

3. Part of your protection plan includes identifying and creating a support system. Write down the names and phone numbers of people you can connect with to help you recover following a triggered moment.

—CHAPTER 5—
THE GRAY THREAD OF SHAME: REALIZE IT IS NOT YOUR FAULT

Then you will know that I am the Lord.
Those who trust in me will never be put to shame.
Isaiah 49:23

If we can share our story with someone who responds with empathy and understanding, shame can't survive.
—Brené Brown

Do you remember the question on little girls' minds during elementary school? It usually came after our mandatory sex education class. Everyone wondered, *When is mine coming?* Then the moment when the girl became a woman, she could say proudly, "My period came!" Many times, there was a word substitution. Aunt Flo. That time of the month. The Crimson Tide. Going to Japan. Checking into the Red Roof Inn.

The initial thrill disappeared as month after month we had to live with Aunt Flo. Every month when she showed up, we could not wait for her to pack her bags and go. If she hung around longer than three days, four days, five days, oh no, seven days, we panicked, especially if we needed to wear white. We developed those slang words because, for some reason, there was silent shame or a stigma when talking about our menstrual cycle out loud. It is a normal part of every woman's life, but we still can't say, "I'm menstruating."

And heaven help you if you were a woman with a heavy flow. You were scared to sit down and scared to stand up after sitting down too long. You dreaded hearing the whispered, "Excuse me, you have a stain on the back of your dress." If you did hear that, you made a mad dash of shame to the bathroom.

Even as I write this, I wonder if this is TMI—too much information. I'm concerned I may offend my readers by talking about a very normal female function of the body. I hope some of you are chuckling as you read this, but I also realize this topic may trigger painful memories of abuse for others. I apologize if it does.

I was stunned to learn how something as natural as menstruation could be viewed as negative and nasty in some parts of the world. I realize it comes from a lack of correct information, but the results of faulty knowledge still cause pain, shame, and isolation for women. It breaks my heart. I just want to wrap girls and women in my arms and comfort them with the truth. Women are fearfully and wonderfully made, created in God's image. When he shaped woman, he called her good. And that's the truth!

An episode of *The Cosby Show* dealt with this subject when the youngest daughter, Rudy, started her period. She wanted to keep it a secret because she felt shame, but Claire, her mom, found out and helped Rudy discover a different perspective. Her mom took her out to celebrate Women's Day. She wanted Rudy to understand and appreciate the honor it was to be a woman.

The Bible tells of a woman who could relate to living with taboo and stigma. Her story of suffering and shame has fascinated me for decades. You may have heard of the woman with the issue of blood. The Bible doesn't say anything of her background. We are told nothing of her family, dreams, desires, goals—nothing. In fact, she is nameless, identified only by her problem. Isn't that true of us? As childhood sexual abuse survivors, it feels like we have no name and are seen or identified by our history of childhood sexual abuse. I want us to stop identifying ourselves by events that happened to us. We are more than our trauma, our abuse, our fears, our failures, our disappointments, our rejection, and our pain.

We have names. Granted, they were chosen for us by someone else, but we get to choose what we do with our name. More importantly, God knows our name. When he looks at us, he sees more than our issues. He sees his creation, his masterpiece. Better yet, he knows us personally. God says, "I have called you by name; you are mine" (Isaiah 43:1). Whenever we are tempted to forget who we are, we can look to God. He knows our name, and he claims us as his own.

I hope you don't mind, but I want to give this woman in the Bible, identified only by her problem, a new name. I researched Hebrew girls' names and found one I believe fits her perfectly. Eliana means "the Lord responded." Surprisingly, Tessa Afshar wrote a novel entitled *Land of Silence* about a woman with a blood illness, and guess what. Afshar named her Elianna too.

The Bible's Eliana suffered from a nonstop, twelve-year menstruation cycle. I don't know about you, but any cycle that lasts longer than seven days is miserable to me, although it may be normal for some people. But if your period lasts ten or more days, you're at the gynecologist's office because there is a serious problem.

For Eliana, one year became two and three and five and so on until the twelfth year arrived. Doesn't your heart just ache for Eliana?

Some scholars believe Eliana's illness probably included iron deficiency anemia. This means she would have lacked red blood cells and hemoglobin to transport oxygen to the tissues in the muscles. Eliana's symptoms likely included dizziness, fatigue, weakness, brittle nails, headaches, shortness of breath, and irregular heartbeats. She also may have experienced dry and damaged hair, swelling and soreness of the tongue and mouth, restless legs, difficulty concentrating, and anxiety. A twelve-year blood loss probably had a severe impact on her emotional wellbeing as well, such as feeling dirty, inferior, and ashamed.

WHAT IS SHAME?

I am sure you are wondering what any of this has to do with our shame as sexual abuse survivors. Let me take you back to biblical times when Eliana was alive. The book of Leviticus gives a detailed plan for women like Eliana, whose periods lasted longer than usual.

> If a woman has a flow of blood for many days that is unrelated to her menstrual period, or if the blood continues beyond the normal period, she is ceremonially unclean. As during her menstrual period, the woman will be unclean as long as the discharge continues. Any bed she lies on and any object she sits on during that time will be unclean, just as during her normal menstrual period. If any of you touch these things, you will be ceremonially unclean. You must wash your clothes and bathe yourself in water, and you will remain unclean until evening. When the woman's bleeding stops, she must count off seven days. Then she will be ceremonially clean. Leviticus 15:25–28

I'll break it down for you. A menstruating woman was considered ceremonially unclean, meaning she wasn't allowed to attend synagogue, the Jewish center of worship, and social gatherings. Anyone she touched, or anyone who touched what she touched couldn't attend either. Jews gathered to worship, pray, and study God's word. The synagogue also served as a social gathering, a place to fellowship with each other, and an opportunity to do business.

Now imagine Eliana's life. No one to kiss, hug, or comfort her with the connection of touch. Remember when in-person church services were canceled due to COVID-19? My heart ached on Sunday morning as I worshipped alone in my bedroom. I missed my friends, the hugs, and singing to God together. Online services helped, but it wasn't the same as worshipping in community. While that season was difficult for us, we still had ways to connect. Not only was Eliana unable to go to church, but her reputation was also affected, her standing in the community was diminished, and her ability to do business was hindered. Friends and loved ones stayed away to avoid the risk of contamination.

Can you imagine Eliana's loneliness and sadness? Her shame, her stigma, and yes, total isolation lasted for twelve long years.

As adult survivors of child sexual abuse, how many years have you lived stuck in the cycle you did not create? Eliana did not cause her illness—she had no control over it. Likewise, you had nothing to do with becoming a part of this select family of sexual abuse survivors.

Like with Eliana's situation, our society also does not provide support or general understanding of our circumstances. When a woman speaks about her painful past, the world wants to know, "Why didn't you stop it?" or "Why didn't you say something or run?" I remember one client who told her mom her stepfather sexually abused her. The mom claimed her daughter was lying, and if anything was happening, it was her fault for flirting with her stepfather. I wish I could say this story is rare, but unfortunately, this theme repeats consistently.

My mother told her grandmother how her grandfather sexually assaulted her and showed physical evidence of the sexual abuse. Her grandmother beat her for "lying." The woman who should have been her shield heaped more abuse on her body and her heart.

Is it any wonder survivors isolate themselves with their painful truths, not expecting anyone to understand them, to touch them, to sit with them, or to connect with them? We learn to keep the secret close because we believe there is safety in silence. Here is the problem with isolation—as our shame thrives, the hope for healing dies. Sometimes we take the risk to come out of isolation by telling someone, but if that person responds negatively, our pain is magnified. This happened to me.

To become an effective therapist, I was required to go to therapy. The idea was for me to experience life on the other side of the couch as a client. John, my supportive and caring therapist conducted sessions for several months. Through therapy, my memory lid eased open as I recalled my sexual abuse past. Not a shock like my later experiences with Mary and Trisha, but more of a wondering. Remembering, I thought John was safe enough for me to share my secret, my shame about the childhood sexual abuse I suffered at the hands of my abuser. My therapist listened carefully as words seeped out of my mouth slowly but surely. My gaze focused on a point over his shoulder, terrified I would see a look of disgust on his face. My words trickled to a stop and silence hung heavy in the air. John cleared his throat, fidgeted in his chair, rattled his notebook, and finally responded by asking seemingly insignificant questions. His eyes looked everywhere but into mine.

"How old was he?"

"Where were you?"

"No one was around?"

On and on the interrogation continued. At last, his eyes connected with mine. Speaking softly, he said, "I don't think it was sexual abuse. It sounds like childhood sexual exploration." He then proceeded to explain his conclusion.

I was stunned. There was nothing exploratory for me at all. Why would I, a young child, want to do anything sexual with a much older person? I could not believe it at first. Then I thought, *Well, he is the expert. He must be right; I must have been wrong all these years.* I exhaled in relief, told him I never thought of it like that before, and never spoke about it with him again.

His response created doubts about myself and my truth.

Unfortunately, I buried the pain and shame deep inside once again, locking the lid tightly until the truth resurfaced during the session with Trisha. In that moment, my pain derailed my defenses. I now know that therapist was wrong. His desire to make me feel better actually caused far more damage. I left therapy with more wounds than I had when I started.

My own experience with therapy is one of the reasons I work so hard to empower my clients. I never want anyone who comes to me for help to have her pain minimized or dismissed as unreal. I don't want anyone who takes the risk to share her secret suffering to leave feeling even more isolated and in shame.

Shame's Role

After my risk to share my pain failed, I quit talking about it. Internally, I blamed myself. *I should have stayed silent. Now my therapist will look at me differently. I made a big deal out of child's play.* When I told myself I shouldn't have played the "game" of exploration, the gray warp thread of shame wrapped around my heart and convinced me there was no safe way to share and get understanding. The core belief that what happened to me was my fault solidified.

Even though I didn't ask to be assaulted and did not flirt with my perpetrator, I saw myself as the villain.

Can you relate? "If I hadn't [insert short blank line], he wouldn't have touched me." The secret message we tell ourselves to make sense of why we were abused—this core belief—feeds our shame as we suffer in secret. How on earth does that happen? Shame claims a role in our lives as it imitates a barrier of protection from rejection. But shame is painful, and sometimes we blur the lines between guilt and shame.

The Miriam-Webster Unabridged Dictionary defines guilt as "the fact of having committed a breach of conduct especially violating law," but it defines shame as "a painful emotion caused by consciousness of guilt, shortcoming, or impropriety" and "a condition of humiliating disgrace or disrepute."

I prefer Brené Brown's definition in her book, *Daring Greatly*. She defines shame as "the intensely painful feeling or experience of believing we are flawed and therefore unworthy of acceptance and belonging."[1] She makes a distinction between guilt and shame. Guilt says, "You've done something bad," or "You've made a bad choice." Shame says, "You are bad." There is a big difference between *making* a mistake and *being* a mistake. Brown goes on to say, "Shame keeps worthiness away by convincing us that owning our stories will lead to people thinking less of us. Shame is all about fear. We're afraid that people won't like us if they know the truth about who we are, where we come from, what we believe, and how much we're struggling."[2] Our shame is fueled by fear—fear of rejection by those who matter to us. Now, do you see how shame imitates a barrier of protection?

Shame tells us it is helping us survive. Like a gloomy overcast sky, the gray thread of shame filters out the sunshine of God's love. The cloudy vision creates a shroud to shelter us from rejection. Reflect on your relationships. Think of times when it seemed someone could be a close coworker, friend, or mate. You wanted to develop the relationship, but shame shouted, "Danger! Rejection Zone Ahead! If they saw the real you, they would walk away and never look back."

Shame says don't take the risk. Shame says stay quiet and we listen. That risk of rejection passes, and we believe we are safe in our shells, but shame has won. We may have missed that one potential hurt, but we have missed out on the connection God created us to crave.

Shame's Restriction

Shame is a barrier to our emotional and relational health. It steals our hope and pushes us from healthy relationships with God and others. On the flip side, shame sends us into unhealthy relationships, because deep down, we think ourselves unworthy of anything better. According to Brown, shame needs three things to thrive: secrecy, silence, and judgment. We tend to judge and condemn ourselves because we didn't run or fight back.

I can hear the cries of protest all the way to my home office. "But, Donna, I just laid there. I could have run, I should have screamed, I should have fought him harder." These shoulda-coulda-woulda thoughts are all faulty beliefs the enemy designed to make us shame ourselves.

I can relate. I remember thinking, *Why am I staying so still instead of running and screaming at the top of my lungs?* Fear raced through my mind, heart, and body. *Move!* I silently screamed. Instinctively, I recognized the threat, yet I remained paralyzed. I blamed myself for not defending myself.

Let's go back to the sympathetic nervous system. Our society views fight or flight as proactive forms of protection.

We take pride in ourselves when we fight back, and we tend to dismiss freezing as an effective form of defense. However, our brain makes the choice for us.

When the portion of our brain called the amygdala sounds the alarm that there is a threat, a signal is sent to the neocortex (the thinking part of the brain) to shut down so energy can be conserved and allow the rest of the body to react quickly. Read the previous sentence again. It is vital you understand this—the thinking portion of our brain stops thinking. We are not consciously choosing to respond with fight, flight, or freeze—our brain makes the choice for us.

The brain then floods the body with cortisol and adrenaline, energy hormones, in preparation to run or fight. But sometimes the parasympathetic nervous system determines we don't have the strength, skill, or ability needed to fight this attacker and run away. So, the parasympathetic nervous system freezes the body and conserves energy so when the attack is over, we will be able to move again. Our brain *makes* our body freeze and submit. The brain also sends endorphins through the body to help decrease the intensity of the pain and reduce the stress.

As victims of a sexual perpetrator who literally overpowers us and takes control of our bodies, we are completely helpless. In that horrifying moment, freezing and disassociating from the present is the best defense left for us. Checking out helps us not to feel the totality of the devastation we are experiencing.

Sometimes, if the prey does not fight back, the attacker may lose interest and wander off, like a bear who tires of playing with a hiker who has rolled into a tight ball. However, if our perpetrator does not stop the abuse, we are better off when our brain acts to lock out what was too scary or too painful to endure.

While that freeze defense so often feeds your shame, I hope to feed your appreciation. You survived. You are here today because your mind protected you in the best way it could. If you're like me, this is a new concept to wrap your brain around. But I want you to practice experiencing the truth of these words. You were not weak because you froze. You were a warrior defending yourself with the tools you had available. My sister, the tool worked, so please release yourself from the shame of using the defensive freeze.

Shame also needs secrecy and silence to hinder our healing. How can we get help if we don't talk about it?

As I worked on this chapter, a gray film randomly began to blur the vision in my left eye. Did I immediately go to the eye doctor for help? Nope. I made excuses. I didn't get enough rest. I used tainted mascara. I don't have time to go to the doctor. I did this to myself with my poor food choices. All the delectable desserts I had indulged in over the holidays and my birthday, I justified, would be counteracted when I returned to my healthier lifestyle. I knew too much sugar could create negative consequences with my health, so I expected better food choices would return my sight to normal.

But alas, the more I reflected on my poor eating choices, the more I blamed myself. I didn't want to go to the doctor to get confirmation, so I suffered in silence. I told no one. I didn't ask anyone to pray. Nothing. Finally, I knew I needed help, and I asked my husband to pray as I made the doctor's appointment.

"How long has this been going on?" he asked.

"Weeks." I whispered.

"What!? Why didn't you say anything?"

"Good question," I responded.

As I pondered my answer, I heard the Lord whisper, "Shame."

I was stunned! Here I was telling my readers shame is a toxic barrier to healing, and I literally let shame prevent me from getting help for my eyesight. Wow! See how quickly lies cause trouble?

When I finally went to my appointment, my eye doctor told me I had a cataract. He saw the film over my eye and said, "Welcome to sixty." Now, I celebrated my whole birthday year, but this was an unexpected "present." The doctor confirmed the diagnosis had nothing to do with my two weeks of poor lifestyle choices—this was a gift of aging. I didn't know whether to feel relieved or insulted. The point is I suffered in silence needlessly, but once my pain became greater than my shame, I reached out for help.

Like my cataract clouding my vision, shame gets in the way of us clearly seeing how much God loves, values, and cares for us. Lies are corrected by the truth. I want this freedom for you, my sister. Don't make my mistake. Don't let shame hinder the healing God desires you to receive. We need to starve shame by sharing our story with someone safe.

When I taught child abuse protection skills to children, I said, "Tell someone until you find someone who will listen and believe you." I had to practice what I taught. My therapist did not believe me, but I kept silent in my shame until I shared my pain with my friend Mary. Her compassion and caring empowered me to take the risk with another therapist, Shelley. Shelley created a space of safety to help me break out of my cocoon of silence. As shame starved, my healing began.

Shame may be whispering these excuses to your heart right now.

- I don't have anyone I can let into my isolation.
- I learned early on I cannot trust anyone with my pain.

- I tried to tell someone; they did not believe me.
- They blamed me or told me I was imagining it.
- I was told I was making a big deal out of nothing.

I hear you, believe me, I hear you. Many women have shared how they tried to tell someone, and things became worse instead of better. I realize I am asking you to take a risk, but this is a burden you weren't meant to carry on your own.

Pray and ask God to lead you to the right person. Tell a small portion of your story to someone who loves you or someone you feel you may be able to trust, like dipping a toe in the water. If your friend responds with empathy and concern, your risk paid off. If, however, your friend questions you, then trust your instincts and stop sharing.

Go back again into prayer mode. It may finally be time to seek professional help. Ask God to lead you to the right therapist. Ask questions about his or her experience working with childhood sexual abuse survivors. Numerous women took the risk to share their stories with me. When their shame was starved of the secrecy and silence, healing began for those women. The common factor is every one of those women broke out of the trap of isolation. If you are reading this book and you are still in your isolation cocoon, I urge you to pray and ask God to reveal to you someone to whom you can speak.

Shame's Retirement

By now, I hope you realize you no longer need to hide behind shame. It was a flimsy protection at best, and it caused more harm than good. Now is the time to retire shame.

Of course, we still need protection because our hearts are tender. The fear of rejection is real, and hope for a healthy relationship is scary. If shame won't protect us, what will?

Good question, and I have an answer. Drop shame's barrier of lies and pull on God's body shaper of truth.

Now that we know shame has been a sham all this time, let's shine a bright light on some of the lies we've been listening to for far too long. We all have a full vocabulary of words to describe our faults.

- I'm not smart enough.
- I'm not beautiful enough.
- I'm not skinny enough.

After a while the negative messages start to hit closer to our hearts.

- I'm worthless.
- I deserved to be punished.
- I don't deserve a healthy relationship.
- It's my fault I was abused.

Now add in the lies we believe about other people.

- I must be perfect, or they won't like me.
- Everyone leaves me.
- No one is trustworthy.
- When they understand the real me, I will be rejected.

The torrent is raging now. Here come the lies shame tells us about God.

- God can't love me because I am unlovable.
- I have to earn God's love.
- God won't or can't forgive the terrible things I've done.
- God doesn't care about me.

My sister, my sister, I want you to lean in closely and pay attention. For some of you, what I'm about to say is something you will hear for the first time. For others, you have heard it, read it, and perhaps have even told yourself, but you still struggle with the truth. Ready?

The abuse was not your fault! I repeat, the abuse was not your fault! One more time, the abuse was not your fault! Nothing you said, nothing you did, nothing you wore, nowhere you went justified what happened to you. You did not wake up that morning thinking, "Where can I go to be molested today?" You did not climb into your bed that night thinking, "I hope someone climbs into bed with me and touches me in ways that I don't want to be touched or does things to me I never imagined."

Some of you may be reading this right now thinking, "But, Donna, you don't know my story." You're right, I don't know your personal story. But you know, and so does God. What happened to you broke his heart just as it broke yours. He wants you free of the lie that tells you it was your fault. God wants you to lay down shame's barrier and pick up his shaper of truth.

Shame's barrier of lies says your identity is "child abuse victim."

God's shaper of truth says, "I have called you by name. You are mine" (Isaiah 43:1).

Shame's barrier of lies says, "If you knew the truth about me, you wouldn't love me."

God's shaper of truth says, "I have loved you, my people, with an everlasting love (Jeremiah 31:3).

Shame's barrier of lies says, "If you knew the truth about me, you would leave me."

God's shaper of truth says, "I will never fail you; I will never abandon you (Hebrews 13:5).

When we raise God's shaper of truth for our real protection, shame must go. No need for silence. God hears us. No need for secrecy. God knows it all. No need for judgment. We serve a compassionate and merciful God. We can say with confidence, "But you, O Lord, are a shield around me; you are my glory, the one who holds my head high" (Psalm 3:3). God holds our heads up high. We no longer need to bow our heads in shame. He reminds us, "Those who trust in me will never be put to shame" (Isaiah 49:23). God's shaper of truth is the protection we need as we continue our healing journey. Check out Jesus's words.

> The Spirit of the Lord is upon me,
> for he has anointed me to bring Good News to the poor.
> He has sent me to proclaim that captives will be released,
> that the blind will see,
> that the oppressed will be set free,
> and that the time of the Lord's favor has come.
>
> Luke 4:18–19

Do you see? Jesus came to bring you good news today if you are poor in spirit, discouraged, and depressed. He came to set free those imprisoned by the lies of the gray warp thread of shame. His life within us removes the blinding lies and opens our eyes to the truth. Living life minimally is transformed into living life fully.

Today is the day for the Lord's favor on you. I know this is hard to hear. I get the struggle, I really do. Jesus wants you free and so do I. Instead of defining yourself based on your molestation, now learn to untwist those gray threads of shame, and recognize God's transforming truth instead. Hang in there with me as I show you how.

Tapestry Truths

- Shame is a barrier that imitates protection from rejection.
- Shame hinders your healing.
- Replace shame's barrier of lies with God's shaper of truth.

Tapestry Tips

1. In your journal, list the ways shame has impacted you. The list should include how you feel about yourself, your body, and your relationships.

2. Identify people you can trust to help you break the secrecy of your shame and come out of isolation. Seek God for the timing and wording of the conversation. Do not force it if you are not ready.

3. Practice self-compassion by remembering the little girl inside you who was abused. God's Word tells you, "Then you will know that I am the Lord. Those who trust in me will never be put to shame" (Isaiah 49:23). Imagine your younger self standing in front of you now. What would you say to her?

—CHAPTER 6—
THE MAROON THREAD OF DISCOURAGEMENT
DEFEAT THE DESIRE TO GIVE UP

Do not be afraid or discouraged,
for the Lord will personally go ahead of you. He will be with you;
he will neither fail you nor abandon you.

Deuteronomy 31:8

Remember the time you thought you could never survive? You did and you can do it again.
– Norman Vincent Peale, *The Power of Positive Thinking*

I couldn't believe it. The day had begun with great anticipation and excitement but now hung as heavy as my sopping wet dress.

See, I had a plan, but all the planning in the world did not prepare me for the unexpected. My family lives in sunny San Diego, but seldom do we take advantage of the gorgeous beaches. This day, we decided to spend time at the shore, have lunch, and go shopping. Since God blessed me to lose weight, I was excited to wear my cute red sundress. But I also wore black leggings. If the waves decided to move beyond my feet to splash my legs, no problem. I would ever so discreetly remove my damp pants and still look adorable in my red sun dress. Problem averted right? Wrong!

Initially, everything went just as I had anticipated. While I bathed in the rays of the warm sun, the refreshing water tickled my toes. The ocean breeze invigorated me, and the warm sand oozed comfortably between my toes as I strolled.

When I stopped briefly to face my daughter, a rogue wave smacked my back and my breath wrenched from my body in a gasp. As I stood paralyzed with disbelief, the beauty of the day swept into the ocean as quickly as that retreating wave. The ocean, which moments before had enchanted me, turned my pretty dress into a drippy mess.

I immediately heard all my negative messages playing in my head. *You should have expected this. You can't do anything right! You aren't cute anymore. Why did you turn your back to the waves?* A stranger walked by and said, "Didn't expect that, did ya?"

My mental tapes continued to play. *See, this is what you get. It was better when you could hide behind your weight.* Behind my closed eyelids, I imagined everyone on the beach was focused on me, and they were laughing. I was the center of unwanted attention. It hurt.

When I declared the day a total loss, my daughter said, "Mom, the sun will dry your dress."

I glared at her and silently left the evil ocean behind as I climbed the stairs to the street. I sat down on a bench and felt water roll down my leg. Remnants of salt clung to my skin, evidence of the disappointing day. I picked up a corner of my dress and twisted it like a dish rag. With a heavy sigh, I shuffled to my car, opened the door, and sat in my waterlogged mess of a dress—miserable, uncomfortable, and dejected. I was ready to go home. The sandy fabric rubbed against my skin—a constant, irritating reminder of my failure to remain cute. Again, my daughter tried to encourage me, but I wouldn't be swayed. This was too tough. I had tried, I had failed, so I gave up. My delighted heart had become a defeated heart. In the instant of that wave attack, the mess of my dress became me. I was the mess.

I wish I could tell you that I quickly turned my mood around, but that didn't happen. I was crushed. I could not move forward. The maroon warp thread of discouragement wrapped itself around me. Maroon is created by blending red and brown. Merging the pain from the red thread of trauma with the frustration of the brown thread of triggers leads to the disappointment of discouragement. With eyes bleak and heart heavy, my face reflected the pain of discouragement.

What is Discouragement?

Let's pause for a second, because we need Webster's official definition of discouragement without my personal picture inserted. Merriam-Webster defines *discourage* as:

1. to deprive of courage or confidence.

2. to dissuade or attempt to dissuade from doing something.

Think about that definition for a minute. To deprive us of something means we have access to it in the first place. That means courage is available to us until something triggers, tightens, and begins the removal of our confidence. We have spunk! We have guts! We have power!

The question becomes, how do we loosen the tightly wound maroon fiber of discouragement and hold on to courage? Before we can loosen the threads of discouragement, we must understand what caused them to tighten in the first place. We must discover the source of discouragement.

Let's go back to the beach. Throughout most of our walk, I watched the waves for potential danger. When I saw the waves come a little higher, I simply lifted my dress. The moment I took my eyes off the ocean, I lost the advantage. That slap of cold water soaked me in familiar feelings of failure and robbed me of my courage and confidence. The happiness fled, damaged by defeat.

To battle discouragement, we must be alert to potential courage thieves. Throughout our healing journey, triggers will fire us back to our messy past. It may be someone approaching from behind, the smell of a certain gum, a dripping faucet—anything that reminds us of the trauma sends us reeling. To protect our courage, we must watch for any situation that could trigger our despair. But how? Let's take clues from a case study of someone else who was caught off guard and lost his courage.

Victorious Until...

I Kings 18 and 19 tell the story of Elijah, God's prophet to Israel. King Ahab's wife Jezebel worshipped the fertility god, Baal, instead of God. Baal was a local god thought to send rain for the crops. Because Jezebel led Israel to worship a false idol, God stopped the rain for over three years.

At God's command, Elijah challenged Jezebel's 450 prophets to a showdown on Mt. Carmel between the one, true God and Baal. Elijah outlined the rules. Each team would prepare the altar for sacrifice, then cry out to their god for an answer. The god who set the wood on fire would be known as the true God. Baal's prophets whooped and hollered to Baal for six hours with no response. Finally, Elijah gets his turn. He prepares God's altar, then pours enough water on top to soak the wood the way that wave had soaked my dress. When Elijah offers a simple prayer, God immediately sends fire from heaven to burn up the sacrifice, wood, altar, and all the water surrounding it. (God's fire even torched Baal's altar.) The crowd goes wild in praise of the one true God. Elijah orders the false prophets killed and then prays for rain. Once again, God answers and sends refreshing rain. Elijah is so excited he runs seventeen miles back to the city.

You would think, after such an amazing victory, nothing and no one could knock Elijah down, right? Wrong. He was scared by one angry, vicious woman—Queen Jezebel. When she learned the outcome of the showdown on Mt. Carmel, she sent Elijah a message.

"You will be dead just like my prophets."

Elijah, defeater of 450 prophets, ran for his life. Not the expected response, right? In the same way that I stopped watching the waves and became drenched, Elijah shifted his gaze from God's power, focused on the power of his enemy, Jezebel, and became drenched with fear.

Unfortunately, the enemy of a sexual abuse survivor can be an intrusive memory that slips in when we least expect it. The flashback is so vivid we lose sense of our current safe surroundings. The sound of footsteps approaching, or a creaking door may cause us to relive painful moments. When we focus on the former power of our perpetrator instead of the victory of survival, our courage flees, and discouragement takes its place.

I remember sitting in my car one day waiting for a red light to turn green. I glanced to my right and observed a man staring at me. He flirted with me. I honestly cannot tell you what he said because I could not hear him. But just that little gesture caused my vision to blur and my heart to pound. I labored for breath. Eyes forward, I mentally screamed, "Change, light, change!" Finally, the green light appeared, and my foot mashed the gas pedal like I was racing in the Daytona 500. I was out of there! Tears filled my eyes as I darted around other cars. I longed for the safety of home, so frustrated with my totally out of proportion reaction. What happened to cause my courage and confidence to disappear instantly? In my traumatized brain, harmless flirting shouted, "Danger!" A man noticed me and because he did, I instantly believed he would hurt me. All I wanted in that moment was escape.

Discouragement says we will never heal, a prognosis seemingly confirmed each time we awaken from a nightmare with our head resting on a tear-drenched pillow (or each time someone looks at me when I'm sitting at a red light).

Listen carefully: There is nothing wrong with running for our lives. Sometimes we need to take an emotional time out. Practice self-care. Do not let a temporary break persuade you to believe the battle is over and you lost. Society portrays running from a situation as cowardly. I say use wisdom as you run in the right direction. I urge you today, run, my sister, run! Run to God who is waiting to comfort you. Run to God who longs to restore your courage from his never-ending supply. "Do not be afraid or discouraged, for the Lord will personally go ahead of you. He will be with you; he will neither fail you nor abandon you" (Deuteronomy 31:8).

Easy to say, hard to do, right? God does not want us to ever handle pain on our own. He promised to be with us. However, many abuse survivors have learned how to struggle alone with their suffering. You may have been threatened with punishment if you told the secret. You may have tried to reach out for help only to find no one would believe you. Running to God takes trust. Sometimes it takes a leap of faith to believe God is who he says he is, and he will do what he said he will do. Eventually, Elijah took his depleted heart to God because he had faith God would take care of him. God longs to do the same for you.

DISCOURAGED BUT...

You may be discouraged but be assured you are not defeated. We recognize the need to heal, to learn to walk toward freedom. Like toddlers, we progress from crawling to standing to strolling. Then suddenly something trips us. Bam! We're back on our hands and knees, crawling. We're tripped by a flashback, a panic attack, or a nightmare.

We sigh.

We cry.

We want to run.

We want to die.

We're frustrated with ten steps forward and five steps back. Crawling is easier, safer. We tell ourselves, "What's the use? I will never be able to stay on my feet." Maybe, but picture a toddler learning to walk toward loving arms stretched out across the room?

"Walk to Mommy. You can do it, baby! I'm right here."

Oh, the first shaky steps. That mother holds her breathe and leans forward, ready to catch her unsteady child. Before too long, that baby girl is walking … until she falls and starts crawling again. Why? Miss Thing sees a cookie and realizes it will be in her sticky hands faster if she does what she knows best. Her mother doesn't worry the baby will never walk again because walking skills take time and practice to develop. Eventually crawling becomes more uncomfortable and less effective, and the toddler becomes a runner. Watch out world!

On our journey, we too are learning how to walk in freedom. Sometimes, we must utilize our familiar skill of crawling when something trips us up. Sometimes, we return to crawling back to check the locks ten times for security, crawling back to pretending, and crawling back to feeling numb. But no child crawls forever, and neither will we. With continued practice, our steps will start again. Step to checking the locks five times. Step to feeling our heart leap with laughter. Step to sharing truth with a trusted friend. Our stride will lengthen with confidence the more we practice. There's one more thing to remember when we find ourselves crawling on hands and knees—use the time down on our knees to pray to the God who will help us get back on our feet again.

Satan wants us to focus on our perceived failures, lack of progress, and traumatic memories. He tries to paralyze us and damage us with the maroon thread of discouragement. God knew learning how to walk would be tough and frustrating, so He sent Christ to serve as our example. "This is the kind of life you've been invited into, the kind of life Christ lived. He suffered everything that came his way so you would know that it could be done, and also know how to do it, step-by-step" (1 Peter 2:21 MSG).

Discouragement directs our focus to what is going wrong rather than what is going right. Discouraged women tend to highlight mistakes and struggles but overlook progress and victories.

Take a blank sheet of paper and draw a black dot in the middle. When you look at the paper, do you see the black dot or the expansive white paper? In the way our eyes naturally focus on details and miss the bigger picture, discouragement wants us to see the dot of doubt, the dot of low self-esteem, the dot of futility, the dot of never good enough, the dot of shame, and the dot of blame.

God's truth shows us the dot is overwhelmed by the white of his presence, the white of his love, the white of his peace, the white of his joy, the white of his hope, and the white of his help.

When Elijah ran, God refueled Elijah's courage. Elijah told God of his pain and discouragement at being the only servant of God. Using a windstorm, an earthquake, and a fire, God demonstrated his power. Then in a quiet voice, God told Elijah to continue the journey. He corrected Elijah's distorted view that he was alone in serving God by reminding him that 7,000 others also served God, not Baal. Although Elijah felt lonely and defeated, he was not truly alone. His courage replenished, Elijah restarted his journey of purpose ready to serve.

What about you, my sister? Are you exhausted, afraid, frustrated? What are the lies you believe right now? Do not allow discouragement to continue to deter you. Use it instead to determine and identify the issue troubling you.

THE BRILLIANCE OF RESILIENCE

I want you to know, in those dark moments, when you are tangled, defeated, helpless, and hopeless, God has placed inside of you a special gift created to combat discouragement. I call it the brilliance of resilience. I like the way that rolls off the tongue. If you're resilient, that means you can become strong, healthy, or successful again. Resilience is the certainty you have the tools to rebound from whatever knocked you down. The American Psychological Association (APA) discusses this concept in "Building your resilience."

"Being resilient does not mean that a person doesn't experience difficulty or distress. Emotional pain and sadness are common in people who have suffered major adversity or trauma in their lives. Resilience is not a trait that people either have or do not have. It involves behaviors, thoughts and actions that can be learned and developed in anyone."[1]

That means we can learn how to use the brilliance of resilience in our journey to healing and freedom. Sign me up!

Many aspects contribute to building resilience, but a primary component is caring and supportive relationships inside and outside the family. "Relationships that create love and trust, provide role models and offer encouragement and reassurance to help bolster a person's resilience."[2]

At this point you are probably thinking, *If I had all that, could do all that, why did I need your book?* Remember, resilience is a gift from God that can be learned and developed. Your healing journey may begin with finding a caring and supportive relationship. If you were abused by a relative or you reached out for help and never received it, this may be difficult for you, and rightfully so. But we serve a God who created us for relationship, a truth repeated in his word.

"Long ago the Lord said to Israel: 'I have loved you, my people, with an everlasting love. With unfailing love, I have drawn you to myself'" (Jeremiah 31:3).

"That's how much you mean to me! That's how much I love you! I'd sell off the whole world to get you back, trade the creation just for you" (Isaiah 43:4 MSG).

"He will redeem them from oppression and violence, for their lives are precious to him." (Psalm 72:14).

God longs to know you and be known by you in a way that creates love and trust. In addition, when you accept Jesus as your Lord and Savior, you become part of God's family. You gain brothers and sisters in Christ—fellow believers—people who become role models and encouragers. Jesus said people will know we are family by the way we show love to each other. Check out God's family rules.

"This is my commandment: Love each other in the same way I have loved you" (John 15:12).

"So then, let us aim for harmony in the church and try to build each other up" (Romans 14:19).

"Let us think of ways to motivate one another to acts of love and good works" (Hebrews 10:24).

God is clear. He desires Christ followers to thrive in relationships that display his kind of love and trust. If you aren't connected with a Bible-believing Christian church family, pray and ask God to direct you to one. In the meantime, spend time in the presence of the one who loves you more than you can ever know. Talk to him through prayer and let him speak to you through his love letter, the Bible. Strengthen your bond with God and allow him to grow the gift of resilience in you.

Other ways to build the brilliance of resilience in your life include the following:

- Avoid viewing difficulties as defeats. Crises, flashbacks, and stressful issues will happen, but we can choose how to respond to each event. It takes practice and time, but we don't have to let these things rule our lives.
- Nurture a positive view of yourself. God's word teaches us to declare, "I can do everything through Christ, who gives me strength" (Philippians 4:13).
- Move toward your goals. Establish realistic objectives and break them down into small, doable chunks. For example, let "I will never be discouraged again!" become "If I am discouraged, I will journal and remind myself this feeling is temporary."
- Look for avenues of self-discovery and recognize your progress. Previously, a nightmare may have kept you in bed all day, but now, push snooze several times and then get up to face your day.
- Practice self-care. Listen to your needs and feelings. Choose activities you enjoy. Taking care of ourselves helps keep our minds and bodies ready to deal with situations that utilize resilience.
- Pray and study the Bible regularly. Spiritual practices help strengthen connections and restore hope. Talking and listening to God is a reminder you are not alone.

These are a few suggestions to build the brilliance of resilience in your life. Choose a few tips to create your own personal strategy. There is no magical way to get around discouragement—you simply must go through it. However, I remind you discouragement is not defeat. It is not forever—it's a moment in time. Do not let discouragement dishearten you, rather, look at it as a pause, an occasion to look around, notice the circumstances, feel the feelings, and activate your plan. Then begin to move forward again.

Satan knows God has a purpose for our lives, but he doesn't want us to live out that purpose. He wants us to make the losing decision I was headed for that day at the beach. Seated on the bench in my dripping dress, Satan wanted me to take my messed-up self home, defeated and depressed. If I had done so, I would have missed precious family time and a delicious chocolate chip cookie on my tongue. I was surrounded by love, laughter, and fun. Unknowingly, the gift of resilience stirred inside of me. Refreshed by our meal, resilience began to erase the fear of watchful, judgmental eyes. Resilience pushed out the frustration and stress and replaced it with the love and joy of family. Hope began to rise, and courage returned.

Later, standing outside the restaurant, I noticed my dress dripped no longer. My day was no longer gloomy, and my heart felt light. My daughter was right. Time, and time in the sun, made everything all right. I was able to turn off the old messages marked "failure" and play a new one called "truth." My dress was dry and sandy, but I was blessed.

Likewise, on your healing journey, resilience grows in moments, phases, and stages. You may experience days or even weeks of relief before finding yourself once again immersed in the pain of your trauma. Like Elijah, you may want to call it quits. Oh, my sweet sister, do not let discouragement defeat you—this is temporary. Tap into your brilliance of resilience. Reach out to God and your community for support and encouragement. You are not alone because Jesus is with you, strengthening you every step of the way. Instead of lingering on what is going wrong, broaden your perspective with God's truth to help you focus on your progress. Time in the S-O-N will bring healing, and you will find yourself set.

TAPESTRY TRUTHS

- Set aside what is going wrong and focus on what is going right.
- The brilliance of resilience is a special gift from God designed to battle discouragement.
- Concentrate on the white of God's help instead of the dot of doubt.

TAPESTRY TIPS

1. The next time you are damaged by discouragement, grab your journal and write the "dot" detailing your pain. Then record the "white" of your progress in your healing journey.

2. Strengthen your gift of resilience by choosing a safe person to connect with this week. Make an appointment and keep it!

3. Read Psalm 34:17-19 (MSG).

Is anyone crying for help? God is listening,
ready to rescue you.
If your heart is broken, you'll find God right there;
if you're kicked in the gut, he'll help you catch your breath.
Disciples so often get into trouble;
still, God is there every time.

4. To whom does this passage apply? What does it say God will do? Spend some time with God in prayer and ask Him to remind you of His promise in discouraging times.

—CHAPTER 7—
THE BLACK THREAD OF FEAR: OVERCOME HINDERANCES TO HEALTHY INTIMACY

Fear and trembling overwhelm me,
and I can't stop shaking.
Oh, that I had wings like a dove;
then I would fly away and rest!

Psalm 55:5–6

Everything you want is on the other side of fear.
– Jack Canfield

Do you know the number one fear in the United States of America? Snakes? Spiders? Heights? Flying? Nope. The number one fear of Americans is public speaking. Practically every time I speak at churches, conferences, or retreats, I am terrified. I make sure I wear clothes that cover my knees, so no one can see them knocking against each other. I imagine you are wondering what makes me get up in front of groups if I'm afraid. (Believe me, I ask myself the same thing every time.) I speak because my purpose is greater than my fear. My passion is to educate, equip, and empower God's people to be what he longs for them to be. Many hurting people do not have the knowledge necessary to heal or thrive. Lightbulb moments in my audience have helped me conquer my fear. I love to see hope shine in the eyes of the listener when the light of understanding clicks on. One woman told me her lightbulb moment was so profound she even shared it with her students.

My fear of public speaking doesn't go away. When I get the call requesting me to come speak, my brain screams, *No way!* But I answer yes because someone waiting on the other side of my fear—someone like that woman and her students—needs my help. God created me to offer that help, and he continues to give me strength to overcome the fear.

To gain victory over fear resulting from childhood sexual abuse, we need to ask ourselves what is waiting for us on the other side of our fear. What is worth taking the risk to fight fear? Perhaps a healthy relationship is waiting. Maybe self-confidence, freedom, or peace of mind will meet us when we push through. I wish we could have this conversation in person. Instead, imagine me leaning in, listening as you answer. Go ahead. Verbalize your response. Now claim your answer to prayer even though you don't see the reality yet. "Faith shows the reality of what we hope for; it is the evidence of things we cannot see" (Hebrews 11:1). Faith is believing something exists without proof and acting on that belief. Fear says relationships are risky. Faith declares healthy relationships are achievable. My sister, choose faith over fear. Faith empowers you to fight fear. Let me show you how.

What is Fear?

The black thread of fear is the final warp thread in the tapestry of our lives. Anxiety becomes a daily black cloud companion to survivors of childhood sexual abuse. Our deep wounds drive a strong desire to avoid pain, so we latch onto fear as though it can keep us safe. Is it comfortable to live in fear? Not really. Many of my clients describe fear like a squeezing or tightness in their chest, like they can't catch their breath. No one wants to live a life full of anxiety, but the fear is familiar, and we take what comfort we can get from that.

Fear is represented by the color black because it sucks all life, hope, dreams, and peace from our hearts. It robs our lives of color and light and leaves us in darkness. When I asked one client to describe fear, he said, "It's like I'm in space where one by one all the stars blink out of existence, and I'm left alone in the dark."

How would you describe fear in your life? Do you avoid being touched? Do you have nightmares? Does the thought of working through the pain cause your heart to race and tears to pool in your eyes? If you are tired of feeling trapped by the fear that holds you captive, my sister, you are not alone.

Of course, we want to avoid anything that feeds our fear, because that anxiety prevents us from living our lives to the fullest. Unfortunately, avoiding the distressing memories, thoughts, or feelings connected to the trauma of our abuse hinders our healing and creates problems in our relationships. Because survivors are afraid of being controlled, manipulated, or exploited, some become people pleasers who will do anything their partner wants while others create a solid barrier to prevent people from getting close enough to hurt them. Whichever is the case for you, the black warp thread of fear hinders healthy relationships.

Effects of Trauma on Relationships

As childhood sexual abuse survivors, we struggle to develop and maintain healthy intimate relationships. Trust is a core component of any relationship, but our perpetrator betrayed our trust and taught us to fear. That trauma causes us to be hypervigilant, seeing danger and threats everywhere. Unfortunately, our fear may lead us to misinterpret expressions, circumstances, or intentions. The thinking portion of our brains will then turn off and hinder control of our emotions and impulses.

Remember the flirty male driver I encountered? That man smiled, and I became eight years old again, looking in the face of my molester. My perpetrator was affectionate, caring, and interested in my words, but then he hurt me. Because of that, any time a man showed interest, my traumatized brain hijacked my thoughts and emotions and told me a kind man would hurt me. Sitting in my car waiting for the green light, a smile turned into a catastrophe in the blink of an eye. My mind painted a terrifying picture. Fear gripped and controlled me. Fear won.

Every now and then, a strange male will stir up the same cycle of worst-case scenario thinking until I take back control. Bless my husband's patient heart. His consistent love and safe actions over a stretch of time broke through my fear barrier and captured my heart. Fear lost when I took the risk to say yes to my man. We won a healthy (not perfect) marriage and family.

I frequently see similar situations as I work with couples. Let's say I'm washing dishes and my husband approaches from behind. He slides his arms around my waist to hug me, but I scream and deliver a backhand as I detangle myself from his arms. What just happened? My brain felt someone touching my body without my permission, misinterpreted the action, and caused me to fight to protect myself, even though the touch was from someone who meant to show me genuine affection, not harm.

Many of my clients say sexual intimacy with their spouse is their greatest challenge. One woman stated she still struggled with this after forty years! My heart broke for her and the countless other women who hurt in an area of marriage God designed to bring couples closer together.

Part of the difficulty stems from the fact that survivors are sometimes unable to remember details of their abuse. If we doubt the trauma happened, we may not seek help, but our bodies vividly remember the feelings associated with the experience. If, during physical intimacy, our husbands touch us in a way similar to the abuse, our thinking brain forgets that we are with the man who loves us. Our hijacked brains sound the alarm and tell our bodies to react as though the abuse is happening all over again. Despite our desire to enjoy intimacy with our husbands, we still feel denial, shame, and fear.

Communication Blockers

This struggle with physical intimacy also blocks natural communication with our husbands. Think about this for a minute: at the time of our abuse, we were kept silent through threats. "Don't tell." Through fear. "No one will believe you." Through shame. "It's my fault." No wonder we struggle to share our feelings about sexual intimacy. It's difficult to explain to our husbands, "I push you away because I am scared you will hurt me," or "When you kissed the back of my neck, I flashed back to my perpetrator." It takes courage to say, "When you touch me when I am not in the mood, it feels like my body does not belong to me. I don't have a say, just like I had no say with my abuser."

Sometimes survivors keep silent because we don't want to overburden our loved one with the weight of our pain or because we're afraid we may lose him. It's even more difficult when we cannot identify the source of these feelings, admit the abuse occurred, or understand why the abuse happened. However, keeping silent also builds an emotional barrier between spouses. The longer we close off our husbands without explanation of what is going wrong, the larger that barrier becomes.

This book is written to victims of childhood sexual abuse, but there is a secondary victim of our perpetrators. That's right, our partner or spouse is also a victim now. Whoever hurt us, hurt our husbands too. Our husbands who love us also watch us hurt. They are the ones with us at two a.m. when we wake up from a nightmare. They are the ones holding us when we experience a flashback. They are the ones who longs to help us but are helpless to know how. They too struggle with hurt, frustration, and anger. In their desire for more affection, they may pressure us for more physical intimacy, not understanding the more they press, the more they push us away.

Let me be clear. I am not saying this to add more shame and guilt for the impact of childhood sexual abuse on your marriage. You hurt because you were assaulted as a child. Your husband hurts because you hurt. When God said the "two shall become one," that includes the good, the bad, and the ugly. Just as you are seeking healing from your past, your husband will need healing too. To be more precise, your relationship needs healing support. Your husband needs education about the impact of sexual abuse on your life and marriage. He needs to understand his feelings of helplessness matter too. And he needs tools to deal with and heal a marriage fractured by a childhood enemy. Perhaps share this chapter with your husband or invite him to join you in marital counseling for starters.

While childhood sexual abuse creates difficulties for physical intimacy, we can't allow it to become the scapegoat of all the challenges in our relationships. Don't ignore current issues such as parenting, finances, communication, or lack of quality time. Physical intimacy is just one piece of marriage, not the whole pie. Also, I am addressing intimacy issues directly related to childhood sexual abuse. If your problems stem from lack of trust due to affairs, addictions, or physical or verbal abuse, none of what I am teaching here applies. That's a whole different book. In any case, seek professional help. Neither you nor your husband needs to suffer in silence. You were alone in your abuse, but in a healthy marriage, you are no longer alone. Dr. Archibald Hart says, "Your abuser stole your childhood. Don't let him rob you of your peace of mind as an adult." I would add, don't let him rob you of your future.

Damaged Goods

Fear also impacts our relationships through a form of body shaming called "damaged goods." Many childhood sexual abuse survivors believe they are no longer innocent, perfect, whole, or worthy. Instead, they consider themselves damaged, worthless, and undeserving of love or having a healthy relationship. They carry feelings of guilt and responsibility for the actions of their perpetrator. This is particularly true when the victim discloses the abuse and is not believed. If she was told her memory was faulty, if she was blamed or called a liar, or if the perpetrator's word was accepted over hers, the wounded child becomes emotionally assaulted again.

These damaged goods feelings of guilt, shame, and responsibility can be particularly acute if our bodies felt pleasure during the abuse. My client, Sarah, describes her feelings this way:

> I thought the abuse was my fault because I did not say no to him. What was wrong with me that I allowed these terrible things to happen to me? I felt guilty because sometimes I liked it when my father touched me, even though a deeper part of me knew it was very wrong. I see myself as damaged goods.

Sarah blamed herself because of her body's natural response to physical touch. This blame belonged to her perpetrator, not Sarah. God created our bodies to respond to sexual stimulation, a natural reaction that we do not control. If I taste something spicy, my tongue burns, and I race for the milk. When I taste something sweet, pleasure explodes on my tongue. I do not control my tongue's responses to taste sensations. Believe me, I understand the confusion of wanting the abuse to stop yet still feeling pleasure. If this is your experience, please hear me. Pleasure during abuse does not mean you consented or wanted to be molested. You did not seek ways to continue the abuse. This truth will take time to break through the lie of damaged goods, my sister, but your body did what it was created to do. You did not choose how to respond.

Satan uses the lie of damaged goods to tear down our self-esteem. He wants our actions, thoughts, feelings, and beliefs about ourselves to be based on that lie, so we'll push away from our husbands. Did you catch the part where I said this is a lie? "You are damaged goods" is a lie from the pit of hell.

- It is a lie that you let the abuse happen.
- It is a lie that you wanted it.
- It is a lie that you could have stopped it or prevented it.
- It is a lie that you should know better than to go into that room, let him hug you, take that piece of candy, believe him when he said he would hurt you or your family if you told.

Lies, lies, all lies. The notion that you are damaged goods is a lie.

Now here is the truth.

- The truth is you did not let the molestation happen. You had no choice.

- The truth is you did not want to be molested.
- The truth is you could not have stopped it or prevented it.
- The truth is, as a child, you could not have known better than to get in that car, sit on his lap, take that money, or believe him when he told you it was your fault because you came on to him.

I had a revelation about my own relationship with damaged goods. On one level, I am learning not to center my identity on events that happened to me. I know it was not my fault that a trusted family friend chose to molest me. Therefore, I am not damaged goods.

However, I still live life damaged. Through God's healing and my own personal therapy, the lies I've believed are slowly being transformed to the truth, but sometimes I still want to hide. I still struggle with being noticed. I still struggle with self-esteem issues. The lie of damaged goods is one of those tangled black knots that steals my focus, but I don't want to stay twisted up in that lie anymore. I want to live the life God intended for me. While sexual abuse is incredibly damaging, I am not damaged goods. And neither are you.

Fear and shame shape our perception of ourselves as damaged goods, but God wants to release us from the fear of rejection that prevents us from moving forward. Once released by God, we can live in confidence that we are whole and complete, loved and accepted by God and others.

SAFE HAVEN

The best news is that God knows our fear and he does not condemn us. In fact, there are 367 verses regarding fear in the New King James version of the Bible. (That means there is a fear verse for each day of the year with one or two left over. How cool is that?)

To help combat our fear, God gives us the precious gift of healthy and safe relationships so we can be seen and known for who we are and not be defined by abuse. In her book, *Hold Me Tight*, Sue Johnson describes three components vital for what she calls a safe-haven relationship—a place of security, safety, and intimacy. This is the type of relationship that allows us to be ourselves without fear of judgment or rejection. According to Johnson, the secret sauce for a thriving relationship is emotional responsiveness. Yes, it sounds like psychobabble, but emotional responsiveness is summed up by the acronym A. R. E.

Are you accessible?

Are you responsive?

Are you engaged?[1]

My sister, these questions are vital to the health of our relationships. God models the loving relationship he wants us to have on earth with someone with skin on. If you can answer these questions yes, congratulations—you have a safe haven connection. A no answer means a lack of security where trust cannot thrive. Let's explore further.

A= Accessibility

Accessibility is more than just occupying the same space or doing the same thing as someone else. It is about being open to one another and paying attention to one another. Can I trust you to be available to me when I need you? This reminds me of a meme I saw featuring Winnie the Pooh and Piglet. The caption went something like this:

Piglet: "Pooh?"

Pooh: "Yes, Piglet?"

Piglet: "Nothing, I just wanted to be sure of you."

We have the assurance of accessibility in our relationship with God because he has promised he will never leave us. "For God has said, 'I will never fail you. I will never abandon you'" (Hebrews 13:5). When you reach for him, he responds. When you call, he answers. "I will call to you whenever I'm in trouble, and you will answer me" (Psalm 86:7). No need for voice mail.

R = Responsiveness

Responsiveness means we can rely on a partner, friend, or family member to interact with us on an emotional level in both good times and bad. Fear says not to depend on anyone else because you will be let down. But we can find powerful comfort when we share life with someone, when they care about a bad workday, celebrate a promotion, and offer soothing support no matter what. Responsiveness creates safety and gives the message we are not on our own in the world. When we experience responsiveness in our relationships, trust is nurtured, and fear is starved.

This is exactly what God does for us. He is the God of all comfort. "All praise to God, the Father of our Lord Jesus Christ. God is our merciful Father and the source of all comfort" (2 Corinthians 1:3). He tells us we are marvelously made. "Thank you for making me so wonderfully complex! Your workmanship is marvelous—how well I know it" (Psalm 139:14). God responds to us because he loves us. "See how very much our Father loves us, for he calls us his children, and that is what we are!" (1 John 3:1).

E = Engagement

This word embraces all those wonderful feelings of knowing that our partners are attracted to us, value us, and want to be involved with us. Engagement gives us the message that we are valued—we matter. Knowing we have someone beside us who is looking out for us means we are no longer fighting to survive on our own.

God longs to engage with us all the time. "Come close to God, and God will come close to you" (James 4:8). We talk to him through prayer and worship. "In those days when you pray, I will listen. If you look for me wholeheartedly, you will find me" (Jeremiah 29:12–13). God talks to us through the Bible. "It is the same with my word. I send it out, and it always produces fruit. It will accomplish all I want it to, and it will prosper everywhere I send it" (Isaiah 55:11). He also speaks to us through others like our pastors and fellow believers. "Do you have the gift of speaking? Then speak as though God himself were speaking through you. Do you have the gift of helping others? Do it with all the strength and energy that God supplies. Then everything you do will bring glory to God through Jesus Christ. All glory and power to him forever and ever! Amen" (1 Peter 4:11).

Fear tells us, "Life is safer on your own." Although we can usually manage the day-to-day on our own, we lose out on so much. Relationships are risky but a critical source of nourishment for our wounded souls. God has set a standard for relationships that are accessible, responsive, and emotionally engaged (A.R.E.). If your closest relationship does not display these qualities, fear is correct. Your relationship is unsafe. Get help!

Note: If you are experiencing domestic violence, get help and get to safety. Contrary to popular belief, it's not God's will for you to risk your life to stay married. Don't settle for anything less than what God intends for you to receive from a healthy relationship. Fear blocks blessings. Detangle the black thread of fear to experience the blessings God longs for you to receive.

TAPESTRY TRUTHS

- The black thread of fear hinders healthy relationships.
- Your abuser stole your childhood—do not let him rob you of your future.
- Relationships are risky, but a critical source of nourishment for our wounded souls.

TAPESTRY TIPS

1. Make a list of all your concerns and fears about starting your healing journey. This may include reexperiencing the trauma, increased emotional pain, an increased need to self-medicate because of the pain, or a negative impact on your relationships.

2. Next to the things you wrote, jot down something you fear more. For example:
   I'm afraid of failing—I'm more afraid of never getting healed.

3. Meditate on the following verse. Write a prayer based on God's promise to you when you are afraid. Ask him to lead you to the relationships he wants you to experience.

> For I hold you by your right hand—I, the Lord your God. And I say to you, "Don't be afraid. I am here to help you." (Isaiah 41:13)

PART II:
HEALED IN GOD'S TAPESTRY

—CHAPTER 8—
THE GREEN THREAD OF COMMITMENT: DECIDE TO HEAL

Commit your way to the LORD; trust in Him, and He will act.
Psalm 37:5 HCSB

Commitment is what transforms a promise into reality.
—Abraham Lincoln

Now that the framework of our tapestry is strung with all those warp threads—trauma, triggers, shame, discouragement, and fear—I'm thrilled to get to the exciting half of the book. Oh, how I wish I could erase the tragedy of your sexual abuse. Since I cannot, let's lean in and discover God's handiwork as he adds healing threads to the workmanship of our lives. As he weaves the brightly colored weft (we are fully transformed) threads over and under, the painful warp threads left behind by childhood sexual abuse begin to disappear beneath his powerful healing touch. God's threads are designed to transform our pain into purpose, our mess into a message, our test into a testimony. To see how God can transform a broken life into a beautiful masterpiece beyond our imagination, let's look back at Eliana, the woman with the twelve-year menstrual cycle.

Eliana's History

Eliana woke to morning sunlight streaming through her window. Rising slowly, she checked her bed for stains and was relieved to find none. Still, the mat was considered unclean because she'd slept on it. Even though the thought of food churned her already cramping belly, Eliana sat down to eat her breakfast—she'd need fuel if she hoped to make it through the day. "I have no money left to pay another doctor. What do I do next?" she wailed. The despair flooding her heart threatened to overtake her very soul until she remembered hearing about a special man named Jesus.

This man performed miracles. A paralyzed man was able to walk. Another man's shriveled and useless hand was made whole again. Crowds of people with various illnesses reported being healed. Someone even claimed Jesus raised a widow's son from the dead. Unbelievable!

Could Jesus possibly help me? Eliana mused. He was surely surrounded by many people. How could she hope to get his attention? Especially since she was unclean. The teacher and everyone around him would be made unclean if she came near. Was there any way to ask for his help without getting in trouble?

Maybe he didn't have to know. If power flowed from him, perhaps there was power even in his clothes. Yes! If she stayed low to the ground and touched only the hem of his robe or a tassel on his shawl, then she might be healed. If she were caught, she had nothing left to lose. Already banned from worship and being near others, even the teacher's anger would be worth it if she could be healed!

She went over her plan to find Jesus. *He can heal me. I know he can.* With her mind focused and her heart determined, Eliana made a commitment to reach for her healing. (Adapted from Mark 5:25-28).

What is Commitment?

Merriam-Webster defines *commitment* as "the obligation or a pledge to do something or to carry out some action or policy." Sounds good, right? Here's what Abraham Lincoln had to say on the subject.

> Commitment is what transforms a promise into reality. It is the words that speak boldly of your intentions. And the actions which speak louder than the words. It is making the time when there is none. Coming through time after time after time, year after year after year. Commitment is the stuff character is made of; the power to change the face of things. It is the daily triumph of integrity over skepticism.

Take a minute to let that soak in. Did you notice Mr. Lincoln did not say commitment was easy? My prayer partner noticed commitment is the "how to" of carrying out whatever deliberate action is necessary to succeed in the situation. If we commit to healing from our past trauma, we will need to continue to work even when it is hard. Let's look again at the verse that starts this chapter. "Commit your way to the Lord; trust in Him, and He will act" (Psalm 37:5 HCSB).

My paraphrase:

Commit—pledge to carry out the action—your healing and control of your life to the Lord. Trust him, and he will help you transform the promise into reality. Until we take that step, healing is a hope, not a sure thing. We need to act. When we do, the promise of healing becomes our truth. So, if we deliberately make the choice to take the steps to heal, we need to trust the Lord to help us every step of the way. He will do it. I am a living witness.

Some may consider the weft thread of commitment to be green because they think of green leaves and grass, and they are reminded of life. But I'm reminded of traffic. Sitting around waiting for healing to magically happen can feel like being stuck in a big traffic jam. Drivers stopped at a red light let their minds wander and start to think about other things. They may be so distracted that when the light changes, they miss their chance to move. (I confess, I struggle a little bit with road rage. I am guilty of saying things like, "What's the matter? Light not green enough for you?")

What is distracting us from our chance to move? We may be protecting our hearts from the pain of revisiting our abuse. Or maybe we don't want to face the betrayal from someone we should have been able to trust. Or we struggle with hope beginning to grow again. Don't be bullied by broken or unstable relationships, poor health, anxiety, lack of peace and joy, the fear of consequences and shame. If fear of failure is the bully that keeps you fixed in place, listen to William A. Ward. "Failure should be our teacher, not our undertaker. It is delay, not defeat. It is a temporary detour, not a dead-end street." My sister, if you have failed in the past, I understand because I have been there. But your healing has only been delayed, never denied. Failure is an opportunity to learn something new and turn it into a blessing.

Remember, commitment means putting action to our hope. The light is green, my sister. It is time to move toward your healing. Time to stop thinking about it. Time to stop dreaming about it. Time to stop hoping for it. Time to commit. Grab hold of the green weft thread of commitment, because green means go.

Last chapter, we learned that fear blocks us from the blessing God has waiting for us on the other side. Commitment means moving past fear to step forward in faith. The writer of Hebrews gives a clear explanation of faith. Faith shows the reality of what we hope for; it is the evidence of things we cannot see (Hebrews 11:1). We turn the key believing the engine will rumble. We flip the switch knowing the light will shine. We watch the sun set confident it will rise again the next morning. My sister, with the green weft thread of commitment, we can step forward in faith knowing confidently that our mighty God will heal us from the trauma of childhood sexual abuse.

Sick, destitute, and defeated, Eliana had no hope for healing until she heard about Jesus. I wonder if she battled discouragement, feared another disappointment. What caused hope to bloom in her spirit? What got her up to seek healing one more time? In that moment, she could have let fear win. She could have ignored the hope that had been crushed so many times before. But Jesus did the impossible. Jesus did miracles. Could he do one for her? Eliana stepped out in faith to transform the promise of healing into the reality of healing.

WHY ARE YOU GOING?

When I travel, I tend to get lost, so I need trusted guidance. I need details before I begin my journey. With the help of countless travel websites, making reservations for a big trip is a self-serve effort these days. But travel agents used to be very helpful in planning the perfect vacation. You could sit down in the agent's office, talk about where you were going and what you wanted to see and do. The agent then developed a custom plan to get you where you wanted to go. When we commit to a journey of healing, we must plan the details to reach our destination successfully.

The first and most important question is why are we going on this journey? My reason for wanting to heal from childhood sexual abuse was my health. As I shared earlier, my long-term obesity was a symptom of childhood sexual abuse. I would lose weight then gain it all back. I thought I had resolved my past, but I still didn't feel safe at a smaller weight. I knew I needed therapy for myself, but I had many excuses not to go.

Then God sent me to a spiritual retreat weekend. We were urged to find an isolated space, read a passage of Scripture, and allow the Holy Spirit to speak to us through his Word. I clearly understood God wanted me to be healed, and he repeated the message to me that it was time to go back to therapy for myself. Don't get me wrong, I did not open the Bible to any particular book, chapter, and verse and find these words, "Donna Scott, it is time for you to go to therapy!" That would have been great, right?

However, I did read these words, "Be careful to do as the Lord your God has commanded you; you are not to turn aside to the right or the left. Follow the whole instruction the Lord your God has commanded you, so that you may live, prosper, and have a long life in the land you will possess" (Deuteronomy 5:32–33 HCSB). In context, these were God's words of direction to the Israelites before they entered the promised land called Canaan. I understood if I obeyed God and went to therapy (be careful to do as God commanded me), then I would thrive (live, prosper, and have a long life) in my promised land, which is healing from childhood sexual abuse.

Eliana's reason was probably her loneliness and physical and mental fatigue. After twelve years of feeling weak and being ostracized from her community, she decided enough was enough. She grabbed the green thread of commitment and chose to go!

Look for your *why* so you aren't tempted to quit. Your why may be like mine, health reasons. Or your why could be a longing to have joy back in your life. Other whys could be the desire to take control of your life or longing for a healthy relationship. Discover your why and go!

What Will It Cost You?

When planning for a big trip, a traveler needs to think about where they're going and what they'll be doing so they can pack the right clothes and bring enough money. Healing journeys are no different. With our why in mind, look ahead to what may happen to us on our healing path. In Luke 14:28, Jesus told his disciples, "But don't begin until you count the cost. For who would begin construction of a building without first calculating the cost to see if there is enough money to finish it?" Before people chose to follow him, Jesus wanted them to start with the end in mind. Our end goal is healing. But what lies between our starting point and our destination?

I remember redecorating our living room. Trying to save money, I tackled the faded wallpaper, browsed through catalogs for furniture, and spent hours looking at paint colors. But when my eyes crossed and my muscles ached, I realized how much time, energy, and money I had wasted trying to complete a project I wasn't qualified to do. Finally, I hired professionals to work within my budget and give me a beautiful living room.

Eliana had to consider significant costs before leaving the comfort of her home. Her frail, weak body may not have survived a long journey. She risked ridicule and the consequences of not declaring herself unclean as she traveled. And yet, knowing the cost, she paid the price because the healing was worth it.

Counting the cost of healing from childhood sexual abuse means considering how the journey may affect us. There will be a price attached to facing the trauma that left our lives in pieces. Some people may not believe us or may end our relationships. We may need to fight through some of our old coping skills, like silence and avoidance. We may incur actual financial investment for the purchase of books and courses or the fee for a therapist or support group.

One guaranteed cost is time, so you'll need to create space in your busy schedule necessary for self-care. When I considered going back to school for my doctorate, my friend challenged me. "What will you give up? Adding the demands of school to an already full schedule, something has to give." Achieving the title, "Dr. Donna Scott," meant sacrificing family time, ministry commitments, and work and even delayed me from fulfilling God's plan to write this book.

In addition to making time in our schedules, we also need to consider how long we may need to travel this road. For many years, I kept a magic wand in my office for those times when I worked with children. I also pulled out the wand to make a point for some adult clients. We all want the miracle of instant healing, and I guarantee at some point you will ask, "Are we there yet?" I'll use the metaphor of transportation. A trip from San Diego to New York takes five hours by plane, seventy-two hours by train, or sixty-five hours by bus. But if you walk, you'll be stepping for nine hundred and fourteen hours! I don't know if therapy will progress slowly or quickly. Everyone's journey is different, so I advise you not to rush it.

What is the price for your commitment to heal? Time? Energy? Effort? To paraphrase the words of an old Mastercard commercial, the cost of achieving your why by reclaiming your life? Priceless!

How Will You Get There?

Now that we've determined why we are making this journey and budgeted for some of the costs, it's time to make some travel arrangements. We need to design a strategy to help achieve our healing goal.

Let's go back to that spiritual retreat weekend where God promised me I would live and prosper if I were obedient. God was not done with me. That evening we had a special praise, prayer, and candlelight service. One of the speakers called out different names to share Scripture or a message she believed God wanted that person to hear. She called my name first and my heart pounded in my chest. "The Spirit wants you free," she said, and she went on to the next name. Here's the amazing part. She had a lot of words for everybody else but only five for me.

At the end of the service, the speaker approached me and said, "God gave me your name first, and he gave me your name last. He wants you to read all of John chapter 8. The next thing he's telling me makes no sense to me, but I know I need to say it anyway. I keep hearing, 'The therapist needs therapy.'" Then she left.

First thing Monday morning, I called a therapist whose business card I'd kept for years and made an appointment. I had my green light. I ran with all my heart, and I'm so glad I did.

As an "unclean woman," Eliana had to break the law to join the crowd and reach Jesus. So, she got creative with her journey plan. Look at the steps.

1. Discover Jesus's location.
2. Determine how to get there.
3. Recognize his prayer shawl out of all the garments in the crowd.
4. Glide her way through the crowd unnoticed
5. Touch her fingertips to his tassel.
6. Slip back out of the crowd unseen.

Without a plan, Eliana may not have found Jesus or been able to reach him. But Eliana kept her grip on the green weft of commitment to follow her plan to heal.

Now it's time to create your customized plan. Consider what resources may be available to you or what habits may need to change. Your plan may have started when you picked up this book, but a licensed therapist also will be helpful to you on your healing journey. I recommend considering therapy if your distress impacts or interferes with your life or you have tried to feel better on your own without results. If you have difficulty managing your triggers, depression, or anxiety, please seek professional guidance. Check out the resource guide at the end of the book for more information.

If you are not ready for a professional yet, I urge you not to strike out on your healing journey all by yourself. God created us for connection and support. Ask him to lead you to a safe person or support group you can trust with your struggle to heal. And if you are involved in an emotionally abusive relationship, you may need to say goodbye to that person.

No plan is effective unless you follow the steps, so don't be like me. Often, when I get directions from my GPS, I decide the computer doesn't know what it's talking about. Then I proceed to do what I think is best and get completely lost. The last time that happened, I lost three hours of my life I will never get back because I didn't trust the process and the plan of the Global Positioning System. Seek God's direction for your customized plan and then follow his directions to arrive at your healing destination. "Be careful to do as the Lord your God has commanded you; you are not to turn aside to the right or the left. Follow the whole instruction the Lord your God has commanded you, so that you may live, prosper, and have a long life in the land you will possess" (Deuteronomy 5:32–33). Listen to him, my sister.

Now is the time to add your first weft thread to your tapestry. The ups and downs of the warp threads need the weaving of the weft threads to form the masterpiece of your life. The weft threads add colors of hope and healing. The green thread of commitment helps you press toward full transformation from pain to gain. Go, my sister, go!

TAPESTRY TRUTHS

- Trust God to provide a path we cannot see to reach a treasure we could never imagine.
- Commitment means putting action to your hope.
- Determine your why, count the cost, and make a plan.

TAPESTRY TIPS

1. Identify your "why." List your reasons for being ready for healing.

2. What do you need to invest in your healing? Time? Finding a mentor or support system? Finances for therapy? Count the costs and write them down.

3. Seek God's guidance for a plan for your healing. "Show me the right path, O Lord; point out the road for me to follow. Lead me by your truth and teach me, for you are the God who saves me. All day long I put my hope in you" (Psalm 25:4–5). Write this prayer in your own words.

—CHAPTER 9—
THE PURPLE THREAD OF PERSEVERANCE: MANAGE SETBACKS TO HEALING

"But the one who looks intently into the perfect law of freedom and perseveres in it, and is not a forgetful hearer but one who does good works—this person will be blessed in what he does."   James 1:25 HCSB

I will persist until I succeed. Always will I take another step. If that is of no avail, I will take another, and yet another. In truth, one step at a time is not too difficult. I know that small attempts, repeated, will complete any undertaking.

—Og Mandino

Eliana's Struggle

Eliana had to be getting close—she could hear many voices nearby. As she crested the hill and caught sight of the massive crowd in the valley below, her knees buckled beneath her. The man at the center could only be the one they called Jesus. Should she go? Should she try to reach him? Could he help her, or would he be as worthless as all the doctors she had tried?

The first doctor made her carry the ashes of an ostrich egg in a linen rag around her neck in the summer. When that treatment failed, she wore a cotton rag in the winter. The next doctor told her to carry barley corn from the dung of a white female donkey. (Stinky, whew.) Another doctor said to crush the gum of Alexandria, a bit of crocus, and alum into wine and drink it. The miracle was that she kept that nasty drink down.

Boil three pints of Persian onions in wine and say, 'Arise from thy flux!' Or stand at the intersection and hold a cup in your right hand while someone else shouted, "Arise from thy flux!" Not even shock treatment helped.[1]

Eliana was ready to give up in exhaustion, but something inside wouldn't let her. *Maybe this Jesus has the answer I need.* Each remedy had been progressively worse than the one before, and she had no money left for another doctor. She lifted her head, straightened her shoulders, and started down into the valley. (Adapted from Mark 5:25–26)

Eliana's determination to pursue her healing despite consistent disappointment baffles me. Doctor after doctor, prescription after prescription, failure after failure. The Bible does not specify the remedies Eliana tried, but according to the Talmud (the rabbinic teachings relevant to the daily lives of Jews) onion wine and ostrich egg ashes were recommended for suffering women like Eliana. For my asthma, I use inhaler medication—nasty tasting, but effective for my breathing. All of Eliana's regimens failed, yet she never quit trying to get well. Despite every failure, Eliana persevered.

Can you relate? Many of us told a parent we were molested, but we weren't believed. Some told a teacher, and nothing happened. The perpetrators may have threatened us to keep the secret, and fear made us silent. Sadly, many victims are blamed for their abuse because they flirted, smiled, or accepted that piece of gum. Utter nonsense. No child entices an adult to hurt her. These negative thoughts are the obstacles which derail our healing.

As adults, we grow tired of the nightmares and painful memories. We try as many solutions as Eliana had in an effort to regain control of our lives. We medicate with alcohol or drugs or food. We learn martial arts, so we will never be victims again. Method after method, again and again, we take five steps forward but find ourselves ten steps behind. I can certainly relate to that.

I wanted to quit my own healing journey many times, especially when I encountered the obstacles of doubt and shame. Since my molestation, I have lost and gained weight many times. Most recently, on a medical fast, I lost over 100 pounds. Within two years, I gained most of it back. In devastation, I shamed and judged myself. But God showed me this wasn't the end of my story. In fact, the weight gain was an opening to show me I still needed internal emotional healing. Maya Angelou said, "You may encounter many defeats, but you must not be defeated." For the first time, I did not default to giving up nor giving in. I have started—no, scratch that—I have continued my weight loss journey, and to date, I have lost five pounds. This is just the beginning, but with Jesus's help, I will persevere.

What is Perseverance?

According to Merriam-Webster, "persevere" means to persist in a state, enterprise, or undertaking in spite of counterinfluences, opposition, or discouragement.

In other words, perseverance is the struggle against all difficulties toward a goal. It gives us the strength and resolve to focus on what really matters. Perseverance is the little something inside that gives us energy to get out of bed in the morning when we would rather pull the covers over our heads.

Perseverance says,

- Take deep breaths. Focus on one moment of time.
- Put one foot on the floor, now the other, and stand.
- You got this.
- Walk toward the door, take your shower, get dressed, walk out the door.
- You can live your life, one moment or one day at a time.

Perseverance is the guts that kick in when we have none. Newt Gingrich states, "Perseverance is the hard work you do after you get tired of doing the hard work you already did."

Members of the United States armed forces who are wounded or killed because of enemy action receive the Purple Heart, because purple represents courage and bravery. Those medal recipients displayed the kind of perseverance that defeats enemies and wins battles. My sisters, every one of us who survived the battlefield of childhood sexual abuse deserves a Purple Heart. Can I get an amen? Now we need the purple weft thread of perseverance to move past that battlefield and learn to heal.

FIXED MINDSET

When we hit an obstacle, how do we find the energy to persevere? In her book *Mindset: the New Psychology of Success*[2], Dr. Carol S. Dweck discusses the difference between those who failed and those who succeeded. She identified two mindset categories that determine how we confront challenges: fixed or growth.

A fixed mindset is described as one in which people believe their basic qualities, like intelligence or talent, are fixed traits that cannot be changed. They see setbacks, challenges, and failures as proof they can never grow or improve their lives. The fixed mindset believes they're simply not enough. For example, a fixed mindset says:

- This is just the way I am.
- My situation will never change.
- I do not have self-discipline.
- I will never heal from my molestation.
- This trauma will control my life forever.

Those with a fixed mindset tend to give up because they are focused on what they can't do. They remain stuck.

Stuck in defeat.
Stuck in failure.
Stuck in hopelessness.
Stuck in pain.

Learned helplessness is a form of fixed mindset that develops when a human or animal repeatedly endures painful, unavoidable stimuli.

In the 1960s (before animal protection laws), one experiment placed a dog in a cage and gave her a shock if she tried to escape. After some time, the door to the cage was opened and the shock element removed, but the dog cowered and refused to walk out. She had been trained the door was unsafe and the cage inescapable. The dog had learned helplessness.

Can you relate to that dog? I know I can. For years, I remained trapped in the cage of my childhood sexual abuse. Despite glimpses of freedom, fear kept me paralyzed. I viewed the man in the car next to me as unwanted attention similar to my abuse. Successful weight loss may have looked like freedom, but it would have exposed me to interest from men who had the potential to hurt me. My weight became my security blanket in the corner of my cage, and I learned that I was helpless to pursue a healthy lifestyle.

What does your fixed mindset and learned helplessness look like? What prevents you from persevering?

Growth Mindset

Dr. Dweck also discovered people who succeed tend to have a growth mindset. While the fixed mindset views setbacks, challenges, and failures as proof of the inability to reach goals, the growth mindset believes failure is a temporary condition. People with a growth mindset believe their most basic abilities and skills can be developed through dedication and hard work, so setbacks become motivation to persevere toward success. Failure in the moment does not mean they have failed to reach their goal.

A growth mindset says:

- This is the way I am, but I do not have to stay this way.
- My situation will never change if I don't do something about it.
- I do not have self-discipline yet, but I will learn.
- I will never heal from my molestation until I take steps to get the help I need.
- This trauma will not control my life forever, because I'm going to use it to make something better of myself.

A growth mindset accepts challenges and failure as a natural, healthy part of human growth, healing, and achievement. Instead of giving up, a growth mindset learns from mistakes, avoids old and ineffective patterns, and looks for another way out of the cage. Persist in continuing to work hard in the face of setbacks and obstacles.

God's Mindset

Though Dr. Dweck doesn't discuss it, I believe a third kind of mindset exists. Instead of choosing between a fixed or growth mindset, God challenges us to use both. I know that sounds confusing, sisters, but let's break it down.

"And let us run with endurance the race God has set before us. We do this by keeping our eyes on Jesus, the champion who initiates and perfects our faith. Because of the joy awaiting him, he endured the cross, disregarding its shame. Now he is seated in the place of honor beside God's throne" (Hebrews 12:1-2).

These verses tell us to focus on Jesus as our help to live with endurance and perseverance. Peter, one of Jesus's disciples, demonstrated the spiritual fixed mindset when he walked on the water. With his eyes fixed on Jesus, Peter stepped out of the boat and took step after impossible step in the middle of a raging storm. When he took his eyes off Jesus and looked around at the stormy seas, doubts flooded his soul, and Peter started to sink.

Before he drowned, Peter looked to Jesus and cried out for help. Jesus pulled him up and together they returned to the boat. Peter persevered and did something the eleven other disciples did not. Peter walked on water, because he kept his eyes on Jesus.

Jesus is also an example of persevering through setbacks. His friends betrayed him, he suffered humiliation and brutality, and he even died on the cross. When he could have given up, he decided the joy on the other side of the cross was worth the pain. He anticipated the tremendous joy of sitting by his Father's side and having a relationship with you and me.

Let's go back to Scripture to talk about the growth part of the mindset God wants us to have. "Don't copy the behavior and customs of this world, but let God transform you into a new person by changing the way you think. Then you will learn to know God's will for you, which is good and pleasing and perfect" (Romans 12:2).

I cannot think of a better definition of a growth mindset. Transformation means change—not staying the same or doing the same thing, but using our setbacks, challenges, and failures as stepping-stones to victory. Focus on Jesus and let God transform you.

There's an old song I love called "I'm Not the Same" by Walter Hawkins. The powerful lyrics describe a woman who felt dirty and trapped but praises God when he transforms her life to one that is clean and free. With an unhealthy fixed mentality, this woman believed her life would never change, and she would never make it out of the cage. But she declares, "I'm not the same because of Christ!" She exhibits both a fixed and a growth mindset when she focuses her eyes on Christ and allows God to transform her.

Let's be real, healing from childhood sexual abuse is painful and scary and sometimes feels paralyzing. No one wants to risk further hurt when it feels safer to remain in the familiar confines of a cage. But Jesus showed that persevering through the pain leads to the reward of healing and freedom. My sister, take your eyes off the past trauma and your present struggles. Look in the Master Designer's mirror and watch your traumatic warp threads disappear as God weaves in the purple weft thread of perseverance. The full beauty of your tapestry may not yet be clear, but you can trust God with the process.

Perseverance Points

We need to apply both the fixed and growth mindsets to defeat our learned helplessness. But practically speaking, how do we persevere when we are ready to give up? Try these tips.

1. Remember why you started. It is easy to forget our goal when triggers send us back into the furthest corner of our cages. Remember, your freedom is outside the cage

door. Find motivating pictures and post them in a prominent place where you can see them daily. Allow the pictures to inspire your fixed and growth mindsets.

2. Care for your spirit, mind, body, and emotions. I talk about self-care often in this book because it is crucial to your healing. Members of the royal family are well-groomed and pampered. You deserve to do the same because you are a daughter of God.

3. Do one more thing, one more time. The purple weft thread of perseverance tells you, "You've got this." So, when you're ready to give up and you can't imagine taking one more step forward, keep going for one more second, one more minute, one more hour, one more day. And when the next day comes, start again.

4. Celebrate your accomplishments. Joyce Meyer said, "I may not be where I want to be, but thank God, I am not where I used to be." You are further on your journey than you were yesterday, so look back over your shoulder at how far you've come. Make a note of every win in your journal and put a happy face next to it. Then celebrate by having a mini party, blowing a whistle, or doing a silly dance. Whatever makes you happy.

5. Focus on daily goals. As you work toward your goal of complete healing, identify a small step you can take today, like applying one tip from the end of this chapter. Then identify another small step you can take tomorrow, perhaps researching therapists in your city. Set yourself up for success by choosing achievable objectives. Your perseverance will be rewarded with each win, and before too long, you will have reached your goal.

My daughters and I painted a large paint-by-numbers landscape together. I struggled with discouragement in the beginning because of the many tiny, numbered spaces. But we kept the sample picture pinned up so we could see what we were working toward. We set aside small chunks of time to work together, and my daughters lavished me with much encouragement. Slowly, we finished the big job step by step. Today that beautiful sunset beach hangs in my home office as a visual reminder of the power and reward of perseverance.

I've never liked the verse at the beginning of this chapter that tells me to consider joy when facing trials. What is joyful about suffering? But when my setbacks, challenges, and failures motivate me to persevere, that's when joy appears. The trials designed to defeat me draw me closer to the one who delivered me from my cage.

Paul said, "No, dear brothers and sisters, I have not achieved it, but I focus on this one thing: Forgetting the past and looking forward to what lies ahead, I press on to reach the end of the race and receive the heavenly prize for which God, through Christ Jesus, is calling us" (Philippians 3:13-14).

My sisters, I encourage you today. When you want to quit, press on to the end of your race. When you experience a setback, challenge, or failure, remember the joy waiting for you. Keep your eyes on Jesus. Let God transform you as he continues to make you his masterpiece.

TAPESTRY OF TRAUMA | 109

TAPESTRY TRUTHS

- God challenges us to have a both a fixed and growth mindset.
- Persist in continuing to work hard in the face of setbacks and obstacles.
- Focus on Jesus and let God transform you.

TAPESTRY TIPS

Time for self-care. In your journal, write down activities you love to do. No limits. If you have trouble getting started, here are some ideas.

- Read
- Take a bubble bath
- Color/Paint
- Take a walk or hike
- Dance
- Exercise (Some people enjoy this!)
- Get a massage
- Get a pedicure and/or manicure
- Go to the movies or watch a movie at home

Practice a fixed growth mindset. What will help you focus on Jesus as you continue your healing journey despite the obstacles?

List your victories so far. I know you have some. You can add "not quitting" to your list because you are still reading this book. Write down the rest of your victories. You may be surprised.

—CHAPTER 10—
THE BLUE THREAD OF HOPE:
REACH FOR YOUR HEALING

And the Scriptures give us hope and encouragement as we wait patiently for God's promises to be fulfilled.
Romans 15:4

Let your hopes, not your hurts, shape your future.
– Robert H. Schuller

Eliana's Drive

Despair filled Eliana's heart as she gazed at the crowd blocking Jesus from view. Twelve years of blood loss had made her weak, but she couldn't quit. She desperately needed a miracle from Jesus. But how could she get through the crushing crowd? The smallest of openings appeared, and she slipped her frail body through, silently apologizing to everyone she touched. Moving precious inches closer to her goal, at last she saw him.

Jesus is within my reach.

Eliana couldn't bring herself to make Jesus unclean, so looked down for his tassel. The blue and white threads flipped back and forth as he pressed through the crowd. She drew a deep breath and crouched down on hands and knees. Her heart beat with hope as she thrust forward and brushed the tip of her fingers under the tassel. Just a soft caress, but immediately the bleeding stopped, and she was healed.

Oh, thank you, Jesus! I'm healed! (Adapted from Matthew 9:20-21; Mark 5:28-29)

Can you feel Eliana's joy? Her commitment and perseverance were rewarded. I imagine that mass of people blocking her access to Jesus must have looked like a Black Friday crowd of shoppers.

I resisted Black Friday sales for years, but my friend talked me into going. Nothing could have prepared me for the madness, the chaos, the noise. Shouts, shoving, hordes of people lined up at three a.m. to get that unique doll, new game system, or big screen television at ridiculously low prices. Now imagine frail, anemic, weak Eliana as she pushed through the masses, slipped, and slid through any tiny crack in the crowd. She mustered the strength to crawl on hands and knees inch by inch until she reached her goal. What propelled her past her fear to get the help she so desperately needed? Hope. The blue weft thread of hope drove Eliana to risk everything to achieve her healing.

What is hope?

Merriam-Webster states *hope* is "to desire with expectation or with belief in the possibility of obtaining." Hope is the yearning for things to get better and the longing for an improved outcome.

During the one-hour drive to my first therapy session with Shelley, my heart beat with hope too. The possibility of healing after decades of dealing with the impact of my abuse made the journey worth it. I longed for the healing my clients experienced. While I did not have to wiggle through a crowd, I did have to face my mild phobia of driving through traffic. Like Eliana, I gathered my courage and faced my fear, because I wanted my life to get better.

The flicker of hope in my heart burst into flame as I took the risk again to share my abuse story, and Shelley believed me. She helped me make sense of my pain while equipping me with new skills. She prayed with me and encouraged me to talk to God and allow Him to join me on my healing journey. Healing from childhood sexual abuse wasn't instantaneous but takes time. My hope for healing became my reality.

Eliana is a beautiful example of someone who took hope in her hands as she fell to her knees in front of a crowd of people who had every reason to reject her. She pushed past the fear of discovery to persevere for healing by touching the hem of Jesus's garment. But why the hem? The sleeve or back would have been easier to reach. What was the significance of Eliana's target?

WHAT'S IN A TASSEL?

In his book, *The Hem of His Garment: Touching the Power in God's Word*[1], Dr. John D. Garr explains the cultural distinction between our modern perception of a hem and the Jewish definition. We think of the stitched bottom edge of clothing as the hem. But when translating the New Testament from the original Greek, that word, *kraspedon*, means the fringe or tassel hanging down from a garment. The Hebrew word for kraspedon is *tzitzit*. Eliana reached for the tzitzit of Jesus's garment because of this command in the Old Testament:

> The LORD said to Moses, "Speak to the Israelites and tell them that throughout their generations they are to make tassels [tzitzit] for the corners of their garments, and put a blue cord on the tassel [tzitzit] at each corner. These will serve as tassels [tzitzit] for you to look at, so that you may remember all the LORD's commands

and obey them and not become unfaithful by following your own heart and your own eyes." (Numbers 15:37–39 HCSB)

The tzitzit was formed with seven white threads (symbolizing purity and perfection) interlaced with one longer blue thread called the shamash, or servant thread, which binds all the threads together. This construction of the tassel was intentional for three reasons. First, in the ancient Hebrew culture, the eight threads symbolized the numeric definition of new beginnings. My sister, aren't we all hoping for a new beginning? Second, the blue thread represented God's throne, which Ezekiel 1:26 tells us was made of lapis lazuli, a precious blue stone. Wearing an ankle length poncho with blue threads around their shoulders reminded Jews that God was with them. And third, using the blue thread to bind the white threads symbolized their hope in God.

Qavah is the Hebrew word for the way these threads were twisted, bound, and woven securely together. But this same word qavah means to wait by binding and twisting yourself in hope and trust. The English definition of wait or hope implies passivity. The Hebrew definition of qavah, however, is to wait actively with anticipation, hopefully watching for God to act. Here is how the prophet Isaiah put it.

> But those who wait upon GOD get fresh strength.
> They spread their wings and soar like eagles,
> They run and don't get tired,
>   they walk and don't lag behind. (Isaiah 40:31 MSG)

Adding the literal definition of qavah, my interpretation and application of Isaiah 40:31 looks like this:

> But those who entwine and weave their lives with God and his Word like a tzitzit will gain their strength and

renew their hope. They will soar like eagles through the storms of doubt and defeat. They will stay committed and not give up. They will tirelessly persevere until they reach their goal!

Sounds good in theory, but how do we practically apply this principle? Let's look back at that blue thread, the shamash. This servant thread is symbolic of Jesus, who described himself as a servant. "For even the Son of Man came not to be served but to serve others and to give his life as a ransom for many" (Mark 10:45). The apostle John called Jesus the Word. "So the Word became human and made his home among us. He was full of unfailing love and faithfulness. And we have seen his glory, the glory of the Father's one and only Son" (John 1:14). God commanded the Israelites to wear the tassel as a reminder to remember and obey God's Word. My sister, we must actively wait for our healing by entwining ourselves in God's Word. Our strength is depleted, but his strength is limitless. Our hope is exhaustible, but his hope is infinite.

God's Word resuscitates and sustains our hope. The Bible says, "And the Scriptures give us hope and encouragement as we wait patiently for God's promises to be fulfilled" (Romans 15:4).

God wants to do that for you. He wants to qavah with you. As you spend time in his presence, he will weave the power of His Word into your heart and fill you with hope and encouragement.

ACTIVE WAITING

It sounds good to talk about hope and keep telling ourselves healing is out there. But what do we do on the tough days? When our hurt feels bigger than our hope, we need something physical and present to motivate us to pick up one foot and put it in front of the other. I turn to the

Word of God. Here are some specific verses that helped me hold onto the blue thread of hope:

Strength: "He gives power to the weak and strength to the powerless" (Isaiah 40:29). I quote this verse when I'm tempted to stop at the donut shop, and God strengthens me to drive by instead. How many times have we felt powerless in our situations? Or the difficulty to get up to face the demands of the day? That's when we reach for the promise of God's Word and his presence to tap into his strength.

Rest: "Then Jesus said, "Come to me, all of you who are weary and carry heavy burdens, and I will give you rest" (Matthew 11:28). When I feel exhausted after trying to meet the needs of my family, clients, and friends, Jesus reminds me to give their cares to him so I can rest. Are you worn out from an unending to-do list too? Tell Jesus your concerns, seek his direction for your daily tasks, and receive his rest.

Comfort: "When doubts filled my mind, your comfort gave me renewed hope and cheer" (Psalm 94:19). When I have qualms about winning my weight battle, God encourages and inspires my victory. I imagine your heart questions your ability to heal from your abuse. Reach for the comfort only God can provide so he can restore your hope and trust in Him, even when the situation seems hopeless.

Love: "For this is how God loved the world: He gave his one and only Son, so that everyone who believes in him will not perish but have eternal life" (John 3:16). When I look in the mirror, feeling unlovable because of my appearance, God reminds me I am loved, not based on my body shape but because he loved me enough to send Jesus. In that moment, I see myself through my heavenly father's eyes and feel loved. If you ever struggle with feeling unloved like me, I prescribe John 3:16 as your antidote. No one, I mean no one, has sacrificed for us like our Heavenly Father. In those moments of pain and loneliness, we need to reach for God's love and receive it.

Salvation: "The Lord is my light and my salvation—so why should I be afraid? The Lord is my fortress, protecting me from danger, so why should I tremble?" (Psalm 27:1). This is my favorite verse when fear tries to rule my heart. When I get triggered, afraid some man will hurt me, God reminds me he is my protector and savior. Let God's light illuminate your dark days of hopelessness with his presence.

Patience: "But if we look forward to something we don't yet have, we must wait patiently and confidently" (Romans 8:25). I need this reminder when I step on the scale and the numbers increase despite my healthier lifestyle. I need to practice patience as I trust God with the process. I don't see the end result yet, but God tells me to be confident as I pursue my health goal. What areas of your life make you feel impatient? We want immediate results. But if we rush the process, the results may be temporary, like my liquid fast weight loss. Now, with patience I am building lifelong skills with lasting results. God wants to do the same for you as you strive for your goal of healing.

Joy: "Don't be dejected and sad, for the joy of the Lord is your strength!" (Nehemiah 8:10). One day, I felt discouraged after reverting to unhealthy eating. Prompted by the Holy Spirit, I did a word study on praise. I was inspired to plug in worship songs and before I knew it, joy flooded my soul as I praised God. When do we need joy the most? When we are sad, discouraged, and defeated. When does it seem the most impossible? When we are sad, discouraged, and defeated. But we actively wait on God's answer to our prayers by wrapping our hearts around his presence and his Word. We may not have joy initially, but we have access to his joy. Then we get the added benefit of strength for the journey. Hallelujah!

Peace: "You will keep in perfect peace all who trust in you, all whose thoughts are fixed on you!" (Isaiah 26:3). Sometimes my mind fills with turmoil as I consider my life's negatives. The flaw is focusing on myself instead of shifting my sight to God. I can't always trust me to get it right, but I can trust him. I exhale my doubts and inhale God's perfect peace. When you wrestle with disquieting thoughts about your situation, try this. Recite this verse, take a deep breath, open the portal of peace, and walk in. Don't walk right back out! Grab a seat and reside there as you keep your trust and attention on God.

Courage: "But as for you, be strong and courageous, for your work will be rewarded" (2 Chronicles 15:7). How do we get anything done without courage? Our hearts may quiver as we confront our pasts but when courage accompanies fear, we find the strength to heal. When we move forward in faith despite our fear, God rewards our courage and our faith.

Healing: "'I will give you back your health and heal your wounds,' says the LORD" (Jeremiah 30:17). When I prepare a new speech, I tell myself to start with the end in mind. What main point do I want my listeners to understand and apply? The end you need to believe is God's promise to heal you. Write, draw, or print this verse and position it where you can see God's promise to you daily.

Why did Eliana reach for Jesus's tzitzit? She reached for God's presence and the hope of his promises found in his Word. When her fingers touched the tassel, her life entwined with God, and she received the victory of healing. You may be saying, "I don't know if this will help—nothing else has." My sister, I will hold on to hope for you. When you look at the blue sky, blue ocean, or even a blue crayon, grab onto that blue weft thread of hope and remember God is there with you. Press forward to Jesus by reading his

Word and use hope to fuel your commitment to healing. Eliana succeeded and you can too!

The blue weft thread of hope symbolizes God's presence, God's Word, and God's promises. He calls us to actively wait, actively trust, and actively hope as we reach for our healing. While Eliana waited, she reached. As she reached, she hoped. As she hoped, she healed. This is my prayer for you.

TAPESTRY TRUTHS

- As survivors of childhood sexual abuse, we struggle to hold on to hope.
- Entwine your life with God to form your spiritual tzitzit.
- The blue weft thread of hope symbolizes God's presence, God's word, and God's promises.

TAPESTRY TIPS

1. God commanded the Israelites to wear the tassel with the blue thread to symbolize him. What is something you can use to encourage hope in your life? Perhaps you can use a blue piece of jewelry or a piece of art that you like. Choose something you can see every day as a prompt to encourage hope.

2. List three realistic hopes for your healing journey. Next to each hope, write down one thing you can actively do as you wait.

3. Personalize Romans 15:4 by rewriting the verse and add your name. "And the Scriptures give us hope and encouragement as we wait patiently for God's promises to be fulfilled."

—CHAPTER 11—
GOLD THREAD OF FAITH: RECEIVE THE REWARDS OF HEALING

And it is impossible to please God without faith. Anyone who wants to come to him must believe that God exists and that he rewards those who sincerely seek him.

Hebrews 11:6

Without faith, nothing is possible. With it, nothing is impossible.

– Mary McLeod Bethune

ELIANA'S BELIEF

Jesus stopped moving. "Who touched me?" he asked.

For twelve years, Eliana had lived a miserable life of isolation and invisibility. Now she wished to be invisible as his eyes scanned the crowd.

His disciple Peter responded, "Master, this whole crowd is pressing against you! How can you ask, 'Who touched me?'"

Eliana agreed. *Please, Lord, keep moving.*

But to her horror, Jesus's voice rang loudly again.

"Someone deliberately touched me. I felt healing power go out from me."

Eliana began to tremble as her miracle became a nightmare. *I have broken the law just being here. The people will hate me. Jesus will hate me.*

Jesus's eyes settled on Eliana. Terror buckled her knees, and she fell in front of Jesus, in front of everyone. In the hush, she opened her mouth to speak. Softly, hesitantly, words began to flow. She described twelve years of devastating illness, useless doctors, and dwindled finances followed by diminished hope and growing loneliness, fear, and discouragement. She longed to shed the shame of being unclean, to touch, and be touched.

"I did not want to make you unclean, Jesus. I thought if I just touched the tip of the tassel on your garment, I could be healed. And I was! The bleeding has stopped."

She kept her face low to the ground, anticipating the judgment, shame, and ridicule from Jesus and the crowd. But sweet words met her ears instead.

"Daughter, be encouraged, your faith has made you well. Go in peace. Your suffering is over."

Astonished, she stood and faced the awestruck crowd, joy flooding her soul.

I am healed and I am free!

(Adapted from Matthew 9:22; Luke 8:43 – 48)

What is faith?

We know that hope drove Eliana to reach for her healing, but Jesus said her faith made her well. What is the difference between hope and faith? In the last chapter, we learned hope is to desire with anticipation. Merriam-Webster defines *faith* as a firm or unquestioning belief in something for which there is no proof. The Bible confirms this definition, "Faith shows the reality of what we hope for; it is the evidence of things we cannot see" (Hebrews 11:1).

In other words, faith is the absolute confidence and trust that God is who he says he is, and he will do what he said he will do. Hope motivates, faith activates.

Eliana thought her healing came from touching Jesus's tassel, but he corrected her. She hoped leaving the security of her home, looking for Jesus, and touching his clothes would heal her. But it was faith that moved her feet down the road, faith that maneuvered her through the crowd, and faith that stretched her fingers toward the Son of God. The immediate healing she received would not have happened if fear conquered her faith.

The apostle Peter explains it this way:

> So be truly glad. There is wonderful joy ahead, even though you must endure many trials for a little while. These trials will show that your faith is genuine. It is being tested as fire tests and purifies gold—though your faith is far more precious than mere gold. So, when your faith remains strong through many trials, it will bring you much praise and glory and honor on the day when Jesus Christ is revealed to the whole world. (1 Peter 1:6–7)

Peter compares a faith that survives suffering to gold which endures fire. But a strong faith is more valuable than gold because it leads to joy. Eliana kept a grip on her gold thread of faith, and she enjoyed the jubilation of healing. Your trauma no longer defines you, my sister. Instead, let your faith be the catalyst for God's transforming work in your life and watch as he weaves the gold weft thread into your tapestry. The painful warp threads disappear as God's beautiful design emerges.

Spoken Faith

Faith is like a muscle—when we exercise, it gets bigger and stronger. One of the best ways to exercise our faith is to say it out loud. Jesus didn't need to ask who had touched him because he already knew. So, what was his motive in exposing her? Jesus provided the opportunity for Eliana to publicly express her private faith.

I don't know about you, but I would have responded with one-word answers and not have volunteered any more than that.

Jesus: "Who touched me?"

Donna: "Me."

Jesus: "Were you healed?"

Donna: "Yes."

Done. Enough said.

But Eliana took the moment to detail her painful path to wholeness. Trembling, she fell to her knees in front of Jesus. She pushed past her fear to share her faith in front of everyone. Can you hear the shackles of shame collapsing from her heart? I applaud her courage.

I remember the first time I sought the courage to share my narrative as a childhood sexual abuse survivor. I should have told my Bible study group of six ladies long ago, but no, I had to be stubborn. Now the Holy Spirit was nudging me to share my testimony with more than one hundred women, and I was truly terrified.

I taught the topic, "Lord, Heal My Hurts," from a mental health perspective. I wrestled, resisted, hesitated, and battled not to get personal about my own trauma. I reminded God my purpose was to serve these ladies in my professional capacity as a marriage and family therapist, not as one of the hurting women. However, the Holy Spirit would not leave me alone. Finally, I blurted, "I was molested as a child." I shared snippets of my story to help those one hundred women know they were not alone in their pain.

God had a word for me too. He said my time to hide in shame was over, because I had done nothing to deserve disgrace. Wow! Words I had spoken to countless clients about shame now penetrated my own heart. Startled, I recalled my client who uttered these painful words, "I am the unspoken broken." I doubted people would see me as effective because of my damaged past, so I kept my past a secret.

Another way to think of faith being like gold is seen in gold-repaired pottery, an artform called Kintsugi. Golden glue seals the broken pieces together and transforms the damaged to the divine. Kintsugi takes broken pottery and makes it stronger and more vibrant, a treasure.

Satan tried to keep me silent about the shattered pieces of my abused life. Adding the glue of faith, bit by bit, transitioned me from broken to beautiful. Faith I am who God says I am. Faith God would help me with my triggers. Faith he would heal and protect me. Faith I can do what he says I can do. The shattered pieces are sealed by the power of faith.

Grasping my faith, I spoke, and my shame began to starve. And as I shed my shame, others were encouraged to do the same. After listening to my tale, several women felt the freedom to reveal their trauma as well. I thought my past trauma would diminish my ability to help others. In reality, the leap of faith I took to share equipped others to share and begin their own healing journey. Trusting God's timing to speak publicly took a lot of faith when filled with uncertainty about sharing my brokenness.

Faith transforms the unspoken broken into the spoken unbroken. Spoken faith is a powerful faith that blesses others as it blesses you.

Is it time for you to speak your faith out loud? Please do not misunderstand me. I am not asking you to grab a megaphone and blast your pain to the world. Unfortunately, there are people who may betray your trust and retraumatize you by belittling, minimizing, or denying your pain. When the time is right for you to speak, ask God to lead you to the right person, someone trustworthy. When Jesus asked Eliana to speak, he was the most trustworthy person in the world to hear her pain. With faith in her heart, Eliana opened her mouth, showed her hidden scars, and revealed her victorious finale.

Challenged Faith

How is your faith right now, my sister? Is it shining like gold refined in the fire of your traumatic past, or has it been dulled by doubts and delayed healing? Are you struggling to trust God because he seems absent during your suffering season? Perhaps your prayers feel like a rubber ball, bouncing on your ceiling but never reaching heaven. In those moments, it seems like applying the gold weft thread of faith to our tapestries is beyond our ability.

If you read Eliana's miracle story above and wondered when your faith would be rewarded with miracles, then I'm with you. I spent ten years praying for a husband. My loneliness intensified as I attended ten weddings without a plus one within a fourteen-month season. I also wondered how I could trust God when he seemingly allowed my abuse. Are you hesitant to put your faith in him to heal you from the trauma?

My faith in God has been challenged on many occasions, my sister. During my therapy sessions, I had to examine my deep wound and ask God directly, "Why did you allow this to happen to me? Where were you?" I trusted God with my salvation, family, and provision. But the wounded little girl inside me struggled with pain, disappointment, and anger toward God.

Joyful Journey: Listening to Immanuel, by E. James Wilder et al., states, "We often question and wonder if God has left us in our suffering. The Bible is clear when it says that God has never left us and will never leave us. He has promised that he would be with us always (Hebrews 13:5). Despite knowing this, we can still feel abandoned due to lack of connection and our prior experiences."[1]

My therapist, Shelley, recommended inner healing prayer therapy to help me share my concerns with God. During our sessions, I invited God to join me in my pain and share my faith struggle. I had difficulty filling my handbag of faith with God's promises to protect or bless me. Shelley walked me through a time of prayer and asked God to reveal my thoughts, feelings, and beliefs about my molestation. Here is an excerpt of one of my sessions so you can get a glimpse of the process.

Donna: "I shouldn't have believed him. I was stupid."

Shelley: "Is that true, God? Was she stupid?"

Donna: (listening for God's answer) "No ... I was not stupid. I should have been able to trust him."

Shelley: "He took advantage of you."

Donna: "Something was wrong with me that he could take advantage of me.

Shelley: "What do you want her to know, God?"

Donna: "No, he was wrong. I should have been safe with him. I had no reason not to believe him. He hurt me. Why didn't God help me? I wasn't worth being helped. I'm on my own."

Shelley: "Is that true, God? What do you want to say to Donna?"

Donna: "In that moment, God was there with me. He helped me survive. He cares that I suffered."

This powerful process of sharing all my thoughts, feelings, struggles, and beliefs with God has bolstered my faith as I feel his presence, care, and love for me. And while I sometimes wish God would create a shortcut to instantaneous healing for me, the way he did for Eliana, I know I'm not alone on my healing journey.

I attended a women's retreat with my mom some years ago, and during lunch, one of the ladies at the table said she did not believe in therapy because God could heal miraculously. I will never forget my mother's response. Up until then, she had not publicly shared her own sexual abuse history. Mom said, "I agree with you, God does heal miraculously. When I became saved, I no longer had a taste for cigarettes or alcohol. People talk about the struggle in quitting, but not me. I never picked up another cigarette or a drink again. However, I have learned while in some situations, God does instantaneous healing, at other times, he will take you on a healing journey. Do I wish he healed me from my molestation pain instantly? Absolutely! But by taking me through a slower process, I have learned more about God and his love for me, and I learned quite a bit about myself too. If God had healed me quickly, there are so many precious moments with him I would have missed. Yes, this is hard, but I trust he knew the best way for me."

You could have heard a pin drop at that table. *Go Mom*! Other ladies quickly expressed their support and encouragement for my mother. And we all would have missed that precious, empowering moment if God had healed my mom quickly.

Those ten weddings were difficult to attend without a date, but I know God never let me go alone. During my seemingly unanswered prayer season, God matured and equipped me for marriage in ways I didn't know I needed. Years after those ten weddings, God did answer my prayer for a husband. This year we celebrated thirty-four years of marriage. I can attest to the fact that God is who he says he is. He can do what he says he can do. He honors his word, and he keeps his promises. Pick up the gold thread of faith, glance back over your life, and look for his presence and his answers to your prayers. Faith is strengthened by evidence of proven faith from the past. God's timing is best in my life and in yours too. Grab faith.

Rewards of Faith

Gifts are my love language. And as much as I appreciate receiving tangible tokens of love from family and friends, my joy is multiplied when I can give gifts to others. I particularly enjoy making my kids work to get the prize buried inside several wrapped boxes or sending them on a scavenger hunt. (You may be able to hear their grunts of exasperation in the background even now.) When Eliana put her faith into action, Jesus's response was a gift. I thought the gift of her healing was enough, but Jesus rewarded her public testimony of faith with powerful blessings packed into just a few words.

"And he said to her, 'Daughter …'" (Mark 5:34)

Eliana is the only woman in the Bible Jesus calls "daughter." This woman—previously named by her illness and invisible to society—testified of her faith, and Jesus elevated her to a family relationship with the Son of God in front of thousands of witnesses. The message to both Eliana and the crowd is clear—she is seen, and she matters to Jesus.

Our identity as childhood sexual abuse survivors was given to us by perpetrators who chose victims. But our true identity is found in Christ. When we choose to accept Jesus Christ as our Lord and Savior, he calls us saved. "For you are saved by grace through faith, and this is not from yourselves; it is God's gift—" (Ephesians 2:8 HCSB). Faith, believing God, is how we receive God's gift of salvation. Our abusers chose to hurt us, but God chose to love us. "We know, dear brothers and sisters, that God loves you and has chosen you to be his own people" (1 Thessalonians 1:4).

Here are a few more blessings we receive when we join the family of God:

- We are treasured (Deuteronomy 26:18).
- We are his daughters (1 John 3:1).
- We are precious to God (Isaiah 43:4).

- We are set free (Galatians 5:1).
- We are new creations (2 Corinthians 5:17).
- We are heirs of God (Romans 8:17).
- We are blessed (Ephesians 1:3).
- We are victorious (Romans 8:37).
- We are his masterpiece (Ephesians 2:10).

When Satan makes you doubt your identity in Christ, wrap the gold weft thread of faith around your wounded heart and believe God.

"... your suffering is over" (v. 34)

Jesus also gave Eliana confirmation of her healing. Eliana's bleeding stopped the moment her fingertips brushed across the tassel of Jesus's garment, but can you imagine the doubts and fear creeping back into her heart every month when her normal menstrual cycle began? I would've panicked. Wouldn't you? If Eliana had slipped away from the crowd unnoticed, her doubts would have traveled with her. But when she testified of her faith, Jesus assured her without a shadow of doubt she was completely, forever, and finally healed. What good news. The symptoms would come every month, but the bleeding would stop, and she would return to normal.

Survivors of childhood sexual abuse often struggle with recurring symptoms and doubt their healing is real. Nightmares and flashbacks may spark our fear, anxiety, and depression, but we have Jesus's assurance that as he heals us, the symptoms will appear less frequently and with less intensity. For some, the symptoms may never go away completely. Wrap yourself in God's presence and his word, utilize the tips offered in this book, and seek professional help to claim God's healing. "Plans fail when there is no counsel, but with many advisers they succeed" (Proverbs 15:22 HCSB).

"Go in peace" (v.34)

Finally, Jesus offered Eliana peace. Our American understanding of the word peace is simply calm or absence of chaos, but the biblical definition of peace is deeper. The Greek word used in Mark, *eiréné*, carries a meaning of quietness, rest, to tie together into a whole. Jesus gave Eliana freedom from the emotional turmoil and physical trauma she had experienced for the past twelve years to relieve her of the unclean mindset. Her crushed life became a life of completeness, without shame or isolation.

Up until this point, we have lived life as the walking wounded, coping with the pain of our abuse. Jesus says to you too, "I am leaving you with a gift—peace of mind and heart. And the peace I give is a gift the world cannot give. So, don't be troubled or afraid" (John 14:27). Give Jesus the brokenness of your heart, and he will use the gold thread of faith to weave restoration into your tapestry. My sister, you will experience a peace that no one will ever be able to take away.

Eliana expected condemnation—she received cheer. She anticipated insults—she encountered inspiration. She expected blame—she obtained blessing. When Jesus called her out, Eliana took the risk that made absolutely no sense. Because she had the boldness to testify of her faith, she no longer had to carry guilt with her. She no longer had to hide her secret or her head in shame. She was seen. She was heard. She was complete. She was healed. And finally, she was free.

Growing up, we sang a song which described faith perfectly. In the song "When the Battle Is Over," Walter Hawkins encourages us not to wait for an outcome of the battle but to celebrate the victory now. Even as we struggle with the trauma of our past, the gold weft thread of faith equips us to shout in celebration. Shout as you claim your healing. Shout as you declare victory over your past. Shout as you transform from victim to victorious. I know you may not see this truth now amid your pain, but faith is believing although we do not see it yet. The gifts Jesus gave Eliana are yours too. Embrace your healing. Enjoy the privileges of your identity in Christ. Put your faith in action and accept Jesus's peace. Let the gold weft thread of faith continue to transform you into God's masterpiece.

Tapestry Truths

- Faith transforms the unspoken broken into the spoken unbroken.
- When Satan makes you doubt your identity in Christ, wrap the gold weft thread of faith around your wounded heart and believe God.
- Give Jesus the brokenness of your heart, and he will use the gold thread of faith to weave restoration into your tapestry.

Tapestry Tips

1. Faith is like a spiritual muscle that needs exercise. We can say like another struggling believer, "I do believe, but help me overcome my unbelief!" (Mark 9:24). One spiritual exercise is prayer. Write a prayer to God describing your struggle for faith and ask him to help you overcome your doubts.

2. Sharing your faith story takes courage. Your story, your words, your audience, and your timing matter. Not ready? Do not share. If you try to talk to someone and it doesn't feel right, stop or shift the conversation. No shame, okay? Ask God for guidance. If you feel led to share, here are some guidelines from "Speaking Out from Within," by PCAR.[2]

- Choose the person you decide to tell wisely.
- Choose your how. Face to face, letter, poems, or art.

- Choose your when and where. Pick a time and setting that works best for you. Your safety matters.

3. Prior to telling the person you choose, make it clear how you want them to react. Tell them what you need—reactions or not, questions or no questions. This is going to be your story, your way. After receiving confirmation from God, complete this statement.

I want to tell _____. I want her/him to know _____ because I need her/him to _____.

4. Write your testimony. I know you have one. You survived. Your perpetrator no longer controls your life. Pray and look back to see how God was with you every step of the way.

—CHAPTER 12—
THE WHITE THREAD OF FORGIVENESS: RELEASE ANGER AND RECEIVE HEALING PEACE

> If you forgive those who sin against you, your heavenly Father will forgive you.
>
> Matthew 6:14

> Forgiveness is unlocking the door to set someone free and realizing you were the prisoner.
>
> —Max Lucado

I imagine reading that verse above sent a shudder through your body. You may be feeling guilty and hopeless. If you believe you cannot forgive your abuser and God will never hear your prayers again, I get it. I really do. I remember wrestling with my anger over the injustice perpetrated against me as a little girl. Like you, I wanted justice. I wanted vengeance. I wanted payback! *How could God want me to forgive him?*

I prayed long and hard about adding this chapter on forgiveness. As followers of Jesus, we *desire* to obey God, but when we read this verse, we *struggle* to obey God. Susan, a participant in The Forgiveness Project, once said "The pressure to blindly forgive, particularly within church teaching, can keep people stuck and unsafe. I believe this easy grace can allow abuse to thrive within families and institutions. I sought help in Christian literature but could only find lovely stories about reconciliation or praying for the abuser's redemption. God forgave me, so I must forgive. This just compounded my sense of guilt, buffeted by a sea of secrets."[1] Susan's words defined my concern. I do not want you to read this book and feel guilty because you struggle to forgive.

On top of that, I was intimidated by the task of explaining the why, when, and how of forgiving what feels like an unforgivable offense. For most of us, our abuser was a person in a position of trust, someone who should have given us security, protection, and safety. Instead, they betrayed our trust when they violated our bodies.

And yet, Scripture repeatedly tells us to forgive. Peter asked Jesus, "How many times do I have to forgive my brother? Seven times?" Jesus responded, "Seventy times seven." As a child, I literally kept a tally of my younger brother's offenses, believing I could stop forgiving him when I reached four hundred and ninety-one. I got to about two hundred and ninety-nine when I learned Jesus did not mean this number literally, but figuratively. Sigh.

When I realized the Lord wanted me to include the subject of forgiveness in this book, I did a little research. I decided to write an afterward because I still felt resistant. Then God had a word for me during a Sunday sermon. When my pastor concluded his series on giving with a message about forgiveness (to my shock and horror), the Holy Spirit made it clear—I needed to pen a complete chapter about the subject.

Forgiveness is never a simple issue, and childhood sexual abuse trauma only serves to complicate the task. But forgiveness is both a therapeutic and biblical issue as we make this healing journey.

WHAT IS FORGIVENESS?

According to Merriam-Webster, to *forgive* is "to cease to feel resentment against on account of wrong committed: give up claim to requital from or retribution upon (an offender)."

The Greek word for forgive, *aphiemi*, means to let go, give up a debt, and keep no longer. When Jesus commands us to forgive, he's saying to let go of the resentment, bitterness, hostility, hatred, anger, and fear we carry toward our perpetrator. That can feel like a pretty tall order if you believe letting go of hurt should be as easy as letting go of a balloon.

In her book *Forgiving What You Can't Forget*, author Lysa TerKeurst explains, "Forgiveness is both a decision and a process. You make the decision to forgive the facts of what happened. But then you must also walk through the process of forgiveness for the impact those facts have had on you."[2] No wonder forgiveness feels complicated—there are two parts involved. One part of forgiveness is the original choice to forgive the events which caused you pain. The second part is the ongoing effort to let go of pain or anger when something reminds you of your trauma. Each time we are triggered by a memory of the abuse, fresh pain floods our soul, and we need to let go again. Part two of forgiveness is hard, but I promise your healing is worth the investment.

When I shared with my daughters about my stubbornness in writing this chapter, my artistic daughter described a beautiful image. When she uses white ink on dark paper, she must apply the ink more than once. The first time, the darkness is still visible, so she waits for the ink to dry and adds more. After applying multiple layers, the darkness is hidden, and the white stands out.

God's tapestry is incomplete without the white weft thread of forgiveness. As we make the effort to forgive over time, he weaves those white threads in until the dark warp threads of our trauma are hidden in the beautiful masterpiece.

FORGIVENESS MYTHS

Now that we know what forgiveness is, let's be clear about what forgiveness is not. There are many myths about forgiveness that we need to dispel before we can move forward.

Myth #1: Forgiveness means you must forget.

So often we tell ourselves our forgiveness is considered incomplete unless we act like the abuse never happened, but God did not design our brains with a delete button. Nor did God not make forgetting a requirement of forgiveness.

Myth #2: Forgiveness means you condone and excuse the trauma.

If the cruelty was all right, there is nothing to forgive. But we were, in fact, injured by the childhood sexual assault. Our perpetrators had no right to hurt us, and forgiveness does not change that. Forgiveness doesn't say there was not wrong committed. Forgiveness says I'm going to choose my feelings about the wrong committed, and I choose resentment will not be among those feelings.

Myth #3: Forgiveness happens when the perpetrator says, "I'm sorry."

Forgiveness is a gift for us, not our perpetrators. So, while we'd all like our perpetrators to take responsibility for their actions and apologize, our decision to forgive may need to occur despite the lack of remorse expressed by the abuser.

Myth #4: Forgiveness includes reconciliation.

Forgiveness and reconciliation are not the same. When trust is broken, it takes time to heal the relationship. If the relationship is not safe or healthy, reunification or continuing may not be possible.

Why Forgive?

God's word commands us to forgive so we can be forgiven, but sometimes we still want to ask why. Why, God, do I have to forgive that person for the terrible thing done to me? Because God wants to protect our emotional and physical health. Yes, you read that correctly. Unforgiveness affects our health.

The medical community classifies unforgiveness as a disease. According to research by Dr. Michael Barry, a pastor and the author of the book, *The Forgiveness Project*, 61 percent of cancer patients have forgiveness issues, and of those, more than half are severe. "Harboring these negative emotions, this anger and hatred, creates a state of chronic anxiety," he said.[3]

Studies have found the act of forgiveness can reap huge health rewards by lowering the risk of heart attack, improving cholesterol levels and sleep, reducing pain, reducing blood pressure, and reducing levels of anxiety, depression, and stress.

God wants to protect us. We may be holding on to resentment, bitterness, and anger to hurt our molester, but that person is unaffected. By contrast, the depression and anxiety caused by our unforgiveness allow the abuser to maintain power over us. Don't let your perpetrator win. God wants you free. He wants you healed. Release your anger and create room in your heart for God's healing.

Not Ready Yet?

The physical and emotional health benefits of forgiveness may not be enough motivation to help with this insurmountable task. Anger and hurt may be a raging fire in our hearts. God understands our pain, and he wants us to be honest with him. That's why his Word includes the imprecatory Psalms. *Imprecate* means to pray evil against someone or to invoke a curse on them. The book of Psalms contains fourteen prayer songs asking God for justice, calamity, or curses on an enemy. I call them the "Get 'em, God" Psalms. God's people cried out for vengeance for horrible acts done to them. You follow me here? Your feelings are valid and understood by God. Check out some of these heart cries for revenge straight from the Bible.

"O God, declare them guilty. Let them be caught in their own traps. Drive them away because of their many sins, for they have rebelled against you" (Psalm 5:10).

"Give them the punishment they so richly deserve! Measure it out in proportion to their wickedness. Pay them back for all their evil deeds! Give them a taste of what they have done to others" (Psalm 28:4).

"Lord, have mercy on me. Make me well again, so I can pay them back!" (Psalm 41:10).

"Don't let them get away with their wickedness; in your anger, O God, bring them down" (Psalm 56:7).

"Let the bountiful table set before them become a snare and their prosperity become a trap. Let their eyes go blind so they cannot see, and make their bodies shake continually." (Psalm 69:22–23).

"Let burning coals fall down on their heads. Let them be thrown into the fire or into watery pits from which they can't escape" (Psalm 140:10).

Can you relate to any of these prayer requests? Read the whole chapter where these verses are found when you have time. Nowhere will you see God shame or condemn the psalmist for his pain, anger, or desire for punishment of his enemy. Instead, the release of anger and pain created room in their hearts for God. For example, notice how David's prayer in Psalm 139 begins with hatred for his enemies but concludes with a desire for God's help:

"Yes, I hate them with total hatred, for your enemies are my enemies. Search me, O God, and know my heart; test me and know my anxious thoughts. Point out anything in me that offends you and lead me along the path of everlasting life" (Psalm 139:22–24).

After David expressed his anger, he asked God to help him understand himself and guide him in his walk with God. In the same way, God gives us permission to be honest about our anger to kick start our healing process.

God authorized the imprecatory Psalms to validate, not condemn, our feelings. Let's be real, God already knows our anger, our sense of injustice, and our desire for revenge. It is no secret to him, so why not express ourselves? Doing so gives him the opportunity to minister to us and eventually help us feel better.

HOW TO FORGIVE

Wouldn't it be nice to wave a magic wand and poof! forgiveness would flow from your heart like Tinker Bell's fairy dust? If it were that simple, God would not have to *command* us to forgive. Remember forgiveness is a challenging, multilayered process which begins with the choice to heal.

When you are ready and feel led by the Holy Spirit to begin the process of forgiveness, I believe you may find these general steps helpful.

Start by asking yourself why your perpetrator or non-protecting parent acted the way they did. Don't misunderstand me. There is never a valid or justifiable excuse for anyone to violate you. But understanding the why may help you move toward healing.

Sally, a former client, experienced severe emotional and physical abuse by her mother, but her mother would say, "Be thankful. My mom did far worse to me!" Sally's steps to forgiveness began when she recognized her mother did the best she could given how she was raised. Sally knew her mom was still wrong, but because she was able to make sense of it, she was able to let go and forgive her mom.

If the thought of forgiveness is still too painful for you, speak to a trusted family member, friend, or therapist for support and safety. Ask for God's help to overcome fear or resistance as you work to forgive the person or people who hurt you.

Lysa TerKeurst described a forgiveness exercise her therapist, Jim Cress, prescribed for her. I wanted to share it with you, my sister, as a first step in your decision to forgive.

Get a pack of white 3x5 cards and a stack of red paper cut slightly larger than 3x5. On the white cards, write specific reasons you need to forgive your abuser, one fact per card. Make another stack of white cards on which you detail specific hurts from other people. Create a third stack of cards with facts for which you need to forgive yourself. Buried in the layers of pain, we tend to blame ourselves, perhaps for not escaping our perpetrator or for judging ourselves for failing grades due to depression from our sexual abuse.

With the cards spread out face up, declare aloud your forgiveness for each offense. Conclude each forgiveness declaration with the statement, "And whatever my feelings don't yet allow for, the blood of Jesus will surely cover," and place a red rectangle over the top of the white card to symbolize the blood of Jesus and his ultimate sacrifice for the sake of our forgiveness. For example, you may say, "I forgive myself for poor grades. And whatever my feelings don't yet allow for, the blood of Jesus will surely cover."

I love this powerful exercise because you cannot forgive on your own strength. You need the power of Jesus and his sacrifice to help you forgive that which seems unforgivable.

I know God enabled me to forgive my molester, but it did not happen right away. I have said before and I will say again, forgiveness is not easy. The acronym F-O-R-G-I-V-E is a process to walk you through the steps of forgiveness.

F - FACE THE PAIN OF THE ABUSE.

My wise therapist, Shelley, says, "You can't forgive until you know what to forgive, so you aren't in sin." Many times, people rush to offer blanket forgiveness before they really understand what needs forgiving, but God asks for specifics before he forgives. 1 John 1:9 says, "But if we confess our sins to him, he is faithful and just to forgive us our sins." If we are going to forgive the way God does, we need to stop burying the damage caused by childhood sexual abuse and start examining the large and complex wound so we can understand what actually happened to us. The 3x5 cards will help with this.

I understand your resistance to this exercise. Though I have witnessed God's power many times as my clients make that difficult journey through their pain and reach their healing on the other side, I was too chicken to do it myself for a long time. There is no way to escape the fact that healing hurts. I am begging you, do not try this step alone. Ask God to show you a trusted family member or friend, a ministry leader, or professional who can help ease the way. The good news is that God is always there.

O - OBSERVE AND EXPERIENCE THE EMOTIONS SURROUNDING THE ABUSE.

Now that we've have made the choice to examine the damage instead of burying it, we need to allow ourselves to feel. Sadness. Betrayal. Anger. Bitterness. Resentment. Shame. Guilt. Blame. Anguish. Again, I caution you not to do this on your own. I also recommend you don't try to do it all in one sitting. Give yourself the gift of time—and practice some form of self-care when you finish. This process can be emotionally exhausting, so you need to refuel.

R - RECOGNIZE THE IMPACT OF THE PAIN AND EMOTIONS OF THE ABUSE.

We talked about this in an earlier chapter, but now I really want you to go back and examine how the abuse changed your life. For example, you may never allow yourself to cry because crying only got you into more trouble. Perhaps the way you dress is based on your assault—you're either all covered up or you're always showing lots of skin, regardless of the weather. Does your anger or your bitterness spill out into other relationships? Do you keep people at a distance so no one can ever hurt you again? When you realize how the abuse has impacted your life, write the answers in your journal and share with your trusted someone.

G - GRIEVE THE LOSSES EXPERIENCED BECAUSE OF THE ABUSE.

The losses associated with childhood sexual abuse can be staggering. Loss of childhood. Loss of safety. Loss of parental figures. Loss of innocence. Loss of healthy love. We prefer to avoid grief because it makes us feel weak, helpless, or vulnerable, but there are no shortcuts on the healing journey.

Like David in the twenty-third Psalm, grief is a valley we must go through—not over, under, or around. Also, like David, we don't need to go through the valley alone, because the Lord our shepherd is with us. This is another step that will be made easier by having your support person at your side. "God blesses those who mourn, for they will be comforted" (Matthew 5:4).

I - IDENTIFY WHO NEEDS TO BE FORGIVEN.

Now I'm going to ask you to do something a little bit different. I want you to identify who you need to forgive. Who was this perpetrator? The parent who failed to protect you? Pay attention to your emotions and the sensations in your body. If the thought of the person you need to forgive sends your anxiety through the roof, then you are not ready for this step. Give yourself permission to say, "No, this is not the time." However, if you can hold the image of this person in your mind without becoming stressed, then you may be ready. This is the part when you take control of your life out of the hand of your perpetrator or the adult who failed to protect you. Control belongs smack dab in the middle of the palm of your hand. Feel it? Believe it!

Perhaps you need to forgive yourself. Despite logically recognizing the abuse was not your fault, you may blame yourself. Possibly you wish you fought or ran from your perpetrator. Maybe you are angry at your body for responding to the abuse, or you feel guilty for not telling someone. Self-forgiveness is the opportunity for you to place responsibility directly on the one who hurt you.

V - Visualize yourself saying, "I forgive you."

With the image of the perpetrator in your mind, picture yourself saying, "I forgive you." Feel free to add anything else you would like to say to your perpetrator in this moment. You might say something like, "You no longer have control over my life. You no longer have control over my emotions. You no longer have control over my thoughts. I am taking my control back where it belongs. You don't have power over me anymore. I forgive you, not because you deserve it, but because I do. I'm letting go. I'm free of you and what you did to me. I am free." Say anything that feels right to you and visualize the power of choice. Take back the power taken from you. Hallelujah!

E - Experience peace as you release.

Take a deep breath, hold it. Now slowly release it, like letting the air very slowly out of a balloon. Now do that again ... and again. Exhale the anger, the resentment, the bitterness, the pain of the abuse. Inhale the peace, the comfort, the contentment, and the relief of dropping the burden of unforgiveness. Remember, forgiveness does not necessarily mean reconciliation or that the abuse no longer matters. Forgiveness means we've released something that held us back, and we're now free to move forward in the protection and provision of God's forgiveness.

When Abby came to therapy for help with anger management, she didn't connect her childhood sexual abuse with her uncontrolled rage. As we processed the pain of her molestation, Abby realized she battled unforgiveness toward her mother who hadn't believed her claim that her stepfather had molested her. After Abby worked through these steps of forgiveness, including the opportunity to forgive her mother in person, other relationships in her life were healed. She was able to nurture and connect with her kids in healthy ways. Most importantly, her molestation no longer controlled her life.

God helped me choose to forgive my perpetrator years ago, but writing this book brought back moments when I practiced the process of forgiveness several times. Because of that continuous process, God unexpectedly blessed me with a special revelation. During a recent family gathering, a relative caught me off guard by asking about my perpetrator by name. Despite hearing his name for the first time in years, I didn't feel anger. I didn't feel resentment. I didn't feel bitterness. I didn't feel hostility. I didn't feel wounded. Instead, I felt peace. I also felt the great blessing of God's timing, since I was in the middle of writing this chapter on forgiveness. As I stated earlier, I knew I had forgiven him but didn't expect to be tested about it. My sister, I am free!

God wants the same for you. He says, "Get rid of all bitterness, rage, anger, harsh words, and slander, as well as all types of evil behavior. Instead, be kind to each other, tenderhearted, forgiving one another, just as God through Christ has forgiven you" (Ephesians 4:31–32). Grab hold of the white weft thread of forgiveness. Apply it several times to the dark stain of childhood sexual abuse. Watch the darkness disappear and watch the peace from the white thread of forgiveness glow brightly.

TAPESTRY TRUTHS

- The forgiveness battle stems from both the desire to obey God and the difficulty to obey God.
- Release your anger and create room in your heart for God's healing.
- You need the power of Jesus and his sacrifice to help you forgive the seemingly unforgivable.

TAPESTRY TIPS

1. Imagine the impact to your physical and emotional health if you were to forgive those who hurt you. What prevents you from doing so?

2. "The Lord is slow to anger but great in power; the Lord will never leave the guilty unpunished" (Nahum 1:3 HCSB). God promises to deal with your perpetrator. Share your concerns and pain about your abuse with him.

3. F-O-R-G-I-V-E. Jot down your reaction to each step of the forgiveness process. If your reaction is, "I don't want to because I'm angry," write that down. God already knows, so he won't be surprised.

- Face the pain.

- Observe emotions.

- Recognize the impact of your pain.

- Grieve your losses.

- Identify who you need to forgive.

- Visualize forgiveness.

- Experience peace.

—CHAPTER 13—
GOD'S TAPESTRY:
PICTURE YOUR HEALING

I want you woven into a tapestry of love, in touch with everything there is to know of God. Then you will have minds confident and at rest, focused on Christ, God's great mystery.

Colossians 2:2 MSG

Overcoming abuse doesn't just happen, it takes positive steps every day. Let today be the day you start to move forward.

—Assunta Harris

Several years ago, my husband called the family together and delivered devastating news. We were facing foreclosure on our home, along with millions of other homeowners impacted by the recession. We went into prayer mode but, to our dismay, lost our beloved home. I remember sitting in church the morning after we packed up our dreams and memories and left our dwelling for the final time. Tears of exhaustion, distress, shame, anger, and defeat streamed down my face. How could God let this happen? I prayed, studied the Bible, attended church, served in ministry, and tithed faithfully. What happened to God's promise that if I tithed, he would open the windows of heaven and pour out blessings I wouldn't have room enough to receive (Malachi 3:10)? Losing our home didn't feel like a blessing—it felt more like a curse!

God continued to take care of us during the following years, but I struggled. I hoped to one day welcome grandchildren to my own home, not a rental. I grieved deeply, but God did not condemn me—instead, he comforted me.

Fast-forward four years. I received a call from our apologetic landlady informing me we must move in sixty days, because she was selling the house. We were losing another home? When I notified my family of the terrifying news, I was surprised to see my daughter whip out a piece of paper to create a wish list for our new home. My faith was depleted, but hers was energized. With this change of perspective, I joined my family in prayer and asked God to provide a single-story home with four bedrooms, two bathrooms, and a fireplace.

Thirty days later, God directed my husband to view an open house five minutes from the rental where we were living. My daughter and I looked at him like he was crazy. We didn't qualify to purchase a house, but my husband insisted on going in. This beautiful home had all the requirements on our list plus a third bathroom and a kitchen that had been newly renovated in my favorite colors. The walk-through tortured me as every room showed possibilities and dreams beyond our reach. Then we went in the front bedroom, clasped hands, and prayed. I left that home (and its dreams) behind but felt refreshed and ready to renew our search, believing one day God would bless us with our own home again.

But God was working on the tapestry of our family's story. I prayed daily these words from Ephesians 3:20 (NKJV), "Now to Him who is able to do exceedingly abundantly above all that we ask or think." And God came through. Against all odds, we were able to purchase that house, and we live in our dream home today. Hallelujah! God answered our prayers and rewarded our faith.

Our tapestry started with the dark threads of pain, fear, shame, abandonment, and unbelievable hurt. Sitting in the church, tangled in those dark threads, I had no idea my dream home waited for me.

Jesus told us there would be trouble in the world, but we never truly expect it. We read stories in the Bible of those who overcame their troubles, and we hear the testimonies of our contemporaries who overcame their troubles. We may even sing, "We shall overcome …." But when trouble comes our way, we immediately complain. Maybe like me, you tend to skip over those verses about suffering. But Jesus reminds us that he overcame trouble so we can and will overcome when our turn to take a stand arises.

You may not be sitting in a church crying your eyes out, or you may not be panicked because a man shows you attention which reminds you of your abuser. But I imagine you may be focused on those dark threads of the pain of your childhood sexual abuse in the same way I was focused on the pain of losing my home. Had I known God was getting my dream home ready for move-in day, anticipation would have replaced my anxiety. My sister, God is weaving your tapestry even as you read this, and your dream of healing is waiting on the other side.

HEALING IS POSSIBLE

God is waiting on you to hand him the green thread of commitment, the purple thread of perseverance, and the blue thread of hope. He wants your gold thread of faith, and your white thread of forgiveness. These weft threads enable God to continue his transforming work in you, his masterpiece.

You see, God does the impossible, but he leaves the possible for us to do. The miraculous healing of childhood sexual abuse is his job. Giving him the threads to work with is our job. If Eliana had not grasped in her hands and heart the threads of commitment, perseverance, hope, and faith, and handed them to Jesus, her story would remain a tragedy. Eliana did the natural by getting close to Jesus. He did the supernatural by healing her body and spirit. The impossible became possible when placed in the master's hand, and the woman once defined by illness was given a new identity in Christ.

My sister, I implore you, do not stay tangled in the messy dark threads of your trauma. Loosen your grip on the thread of shame. Don't let discouragement continue to detain you. Above all else, do not let fear tie down your ability to move forward in faith.

Let's shift our gaze from the confusing mess on the backside of the tapestry to the mirror of God's word and find the beautiful masterpiece God is creating out of our lives. His Word says, "For we are God's masterpiece. He has created us anew in Christ Jesus, so we can do the good things he planned for us long ago" (Ephesians 2:10). If you find that hard to believe, substitute "we" for "I" and say that verse out loud. Go ahead, don't be shy. "For I am God's masterpiece. He has created me anew in Christ Jesus so I can do the good things he planned for me long ago."

Sometimes we struggle to trust this truth because we define ourselves by our abuse and other painful experiences. But God sees you as a fine work of art—even if you do not. When you accepted Jesus Christ as your

Lord and Savior, you joined the family of God. As God's daughters, we are privileged to ask him anything in his will (1 John 5:14). Ask him for your healing, and hand him the weft—We Experience Full Transformation—threads. As he weaves your commitment, perseverance, hope, faith, and forgiveness over and under the traumatic warp threads caused by childhood sexual abuse, watch your life transform into God's masterpiece.

FIND PURPOSE

There is another important part of God's Word I don't want you to miss. From the beginning of time, God planned good things for us, but Satan used sexual abuse to try to derail God's purpose. Now God wants to create a masterpiece from that mess of our abuse.

Are you still struggling to believe God can bring beauty from ashes? Let me tell you about someone else from the Bible who suffered betrayal and abuse at the hands of loved ones. The last fourteen chapters of Genesis tell the story of Joseph, a man who did not experience sexual abuse but was hurt deeply by loved ones.

Though sons of a wealthy man, Joseph's jealous brothers sold him into slavery. There he endured oppression and spent thirteen years in prison for a crime he didn't commit. Through a series of God-sized miracles, Joseph became the second-highest ruler of Egypt.

When a famine gripped the entire region, Joseph's brothers went to Egypt for food and found the brother they thought was dead. They feared Joseph would exact his revenge, but Joseph replied, "You intended to harm me, but God intended it all for good. He brought me to this position so I could save the lives of many people" (Genesis 50:20).

God took the tangles of Joseph's life, caused by his brothers' hurtful actions, and created a tapestry to deliver his people from starvation. We can apply the meaning of Joseph's words to our own lives. We can say to Satan, "You intended to hurt me through the abuse I suffered so I would not be able to fulfill God's plans for my life. Instead, God is making a beautiful tapestry out of that ugly story and will use my message to inspire and help others."

I know it's hard to see beauty through the scars covering our damaged hearts. Our eyes are drawn to the tangled threads on the messy, complicated side of our tapestry. But when we zoom out our focus and take God's view, we can see a tapestry forming—an inspirational and encouraging masterpiece that will help others shift their view from a few tangled warp threads to the many bright colors God is weaving in.

Eliana's tapestry is displayed in the ninth chapter of Matthew. Several chapters later, we read that the people in the crowd "were begging Him that they might only touch the tassel on His robe. And as many as touched it were made perfectly well" (Matthew 14:36 HCSB). I'm not sure if these people knew Eliana's story or not, but wouldn't it be cool if they were inspired by her testimony and reached for their healing the same way she had reached for hers?

When Eliana shared her story publicly, she couldn't have known how her courage would impact the lives of others. I believe our stories can have the same effect on those around us. If we can push our pain into our purpose, God can move our tapestries from dark, hidden secrets to openly displayed messages of hope. We can grow from guilt to guiltless, shift from shame to self-respect. And we can help others move from victim to victorious as well. The apostle Paul confirms, "No, despite all these things, overwhelming victory is ours through Christ, who loved us" (Romans 8:37).

I remember reading this verse one morning during my quiet time, unaware of how desperately I would soon need its comfort and assurance. Only a few hours later, I was in an ambulance en route to the hospital following a traumatizing car accident. As I lay on the bed weeping, the Holy Spirit reminded me that in all these things I was victorious. That concept confused me. How could I be victorious in these things?

The Holy Spirit then whispered to me. "These things—your second traumatic car accident, ambulance ride, additional health injuries, totaled minivan. You are more victorious through me because I love you. You will be all right."

Peace washed over me in that ambulance.

My sister, may I whisper in your ear for a moment? These things: sexual abuse as a child, betrayal, rejection, guilt, shame, anxiety, depression, broken relationships. Yes, you have suffered and felt defenseless, but now you have skills to overcome your past. Look with me as I lift my eyes from the messy back of your tapestry to the mirror reflecting the beautiful masterpiece God is creating of your life.

You are no longer twisted by trauma but committed to your healing.

You are no longer trapped by triggers because you persevered.

You are no longer damaged by discouragement because you hold on to hope.

You no longer suffer shame because you have the shield of faith.

You are no longer held captive by fear because you experience the freedom of forgiveness.

You are loved by the One who gave His life so you can live. God hears your unspoken broken, and he will heal you. My sister, please allow your heavenly Father to weave a tapestry of love with the tatters of your hurting heart, so you can display the beautiful story of his healing peace in your life. Then your story will become his masterpiece.

TAPESTRY TRUTHS

- Tapestries display spiritual and expressive messages to the viewers.
- Reach for the colorful threads which have the potential to change your life forever.
- You are more than victorious through Christ Jesus who loves you.

TAPESTRY TIPS

As you continue your healing journey, childhood sexual abuse will remain part of your tapestry, but I pray its effects have begun to diminish as you practice your tapestry tips. Completion of this book does not mean your healing is complete. You may need to take a break, reread the book several times, or seek professional help. Whatever lies ahead for you, reward yourself for your hard work so far. Celebrate your achievement with something that brings you pleasure. Write down your reward with a deadline to make sure you honor your accomplishments. Feel free to choose more than one!

Live boldly in your new freedom as God's masterpiece!

ABOUT THE AUTHOR

Donna Scott is a licensed marriage and family therapist, who combines her professional experience and training with compassion and insight from God's Word. With over thirty years of experience providing Christian counseling, Donna is passionate to help those with hurting hearts heal.

As a speaker, Donna engages her listeners with her dynamic visual demonstrations and provides tangible, practical tools designed to improve relationships and quality of life. Her desire is to live a life worthy of the calling she has received from God.

Donna lives in San Diego, California with her family.
You can connect with Donna via:
Website: www.donnascottttherapy.com
(Click on Speaking to request Donna speak at your event.)

Facebook: https://www.facebook.com/donna.s.scott/
Instagram: https://www.instagram.com/donnascott.therapy/

APPENDIX A

POSSIBLE SYMPTOMS OF TRAUMA

Psychological/Behavioral Effects

- Dissociation, or feeling detached, confused, or like you observe life more than live it
- Difficulty trusting yourself or trusting others too much
- Difficulty setting boundaries in relationships
- Flashbacks triggered by sight, smell, taste, sound, or touch
- Self-medicating with drugs, alcohol, or other addictions
- Low self-esteem
- Isolation
- Fear of intimacy
- Promiscuous sexual activity
- Suicidal thoughts or self-injury
- Eating disorders
- Sexual dysfunction, pain, or a lack of interest or pleasure in sex
- As an adult survivor, being a magnet to repeat victimizations
- Anxiety or panic attacks
- Fear of medical procedures (Those dreaded pap smear exams, ugh!)

Emotional Effects

- Grieving or mourning the loss of innocence and betrayal by the perpetrator
- Guilt because you possibly experienced physical pleasure at the time of the abuse or received some type of reward, i.e., affection, candy, preferential treatment
- Shame and feeling as though the abuse were your fault
- Depression and anxiety
- Anger or unexplainable rage

Physical Effects

- Gastrointestinal distress, nausea, and chronic pelvic pain
- Headaches
- Asthma and/or breathing problems
- Unreleased stress leading to back or skeletal pain
- Addictions such as smoking, alcohol, and food leading to obesity
- Severe gag reflex even when nothing is in the mouth

APPENDIX B

THE ARMOR OF GOD

To encourage early Christians to fight against the devil using the weapons and armor God provided, the apostle Paul described a Roman centurion's armor. He knew this image, seen daily in their city, would be familiar to his readers. Like that worn by our police forces, the centurion's protective gear and weapons were easily identified. I want you to connect with images we see daily. For our purposes, I think of it more as dressing for success to better manage our triggers.

THE BODY SHAPER OF TRUTH

"Stand your ground, putting on the belt of truth" (Ephesians 6:14).

Paul's description of God's armor begins with the foundational piece necessary for protection. The belt (also known as a girdle) tied around the waist to hold the soldier's clothes together and carry the weight of his armor. Without a belt, he would have nothing to hold the rest of his protection.

As part of our safety plan against triggers, we need God's truth first to hold everything in place as we go into battle. Nowadays, we women go into battle with different attire. Instead of a belt, I think of the body shaper called Spanx. A modern girdle, Spanx has become vital as a solid foundational undergarment. (And the creator has become a billionaire!) Ladies, understand we need something strong enough and secure enough to hold everything in place. Can I get an amen?

When we get triggered, we may think, "I can't take it anymore, I will never get better." When we are dressed in our spiritual shaper, we will feel God's truth supporting us. we'll be able to counter the lie with a truth like, "I can do everything through Christ, who gives me strength" (Philippians 4:13).

I also encourage you to acknowledge the truth of the trigger. Many times, we want to act like the abuse never happened and push it back down. Nope, the memory will come back even stronger. Look your trigger in the eye, acknowledge its presence, and rest in God's strength instead of trying to run away.

Identify the source of your trigger. Was it a sight, smell, sound, touch, or taste? Recognize your emotional reaction as soon as you begin to feel it. Then take charge of your emotions by shifting your focus. Try deep breathing or relaxation exercises, whatever works for you, and practice during non-triggered times. Equip your body and mind to use the updated defense system. To take control back from the triggers. Focus on God's truth. You are safe. No one can hurt you. Claim one of God's many promises, like "If your heart is broken, you'll find GOD right there; if you're kicked in the gut, he'll help you catch your breath" (Psalm 34:18 MSG). You've got this, my sister, because the truth is God's got you.

THE BRA OF RIGHTEOUSNESS

"And the body armor of God's righteousness" (Ephesians 6:14).

The centurion's body armor (also known as the breastplate) protected the chest area, covering vital organs like his heart. Proverbs 4:23 tells us to guard our hearts. We don't use breastplates today, but women need to lift, support, and protect the girls. The sisters at Spanx even created the Bra-llelujah, a bra so comfortable, a woman would say, "Hallelujah!"

But how can a bra of righteousness provide protection?

Righteousness means a right relationship with God. When we accept Jesus as Lord, his righteousness becomes our righteousness. "For God made Christ, who never sinned, to be the offering for our sin, so that we could be made right with God through Christ" (2 Corinthians 5:21). (This verse refers to the sin we are born with thanks to Adam and Eve, not the abuse sin which hurt us.) Triggers tend to make us feel powerless, like we lack control over what happens to our heart, body, and mind. But like a great bra gives us peace of mind that everything is safe, God's righteousness protects our hearts when triggers try to hijack our mind or emotions. And when we have a right relationship with him, he is waiting for us to turn to him for help.

God will lift your discouraged heart. "But those who trust in the Lord will find new strength. They will soar high on wings like eagles. They will run and not grow weary. They will walk and not faint" (Isaiah 40:31).

God will comfort your wounded heart. "Now let your unfailing love comfort me, just as you promised me, your servant" (Psalm 119:76).

God will support your struggling heart. "Even there your hand will guide me, and your strength will support me" (Psalm 139:10).

Shout hallelujah for your bra of righteousness.

THE SHOES OF PEACE

"For shoes, put on the peace that comes from the Good News" (Ephesians 6:15).

The most significant part of the Roman soldier's sandal was the sole, which had nails underneath like football cleats to safeguard the soldiers' feet as they walked. The enemy would throw stuff on the ground to make it difficult for the soldiers to walk, much less fight and win a battle. The nails under the sandals helped them grip the ground. Whether sloped or slippery, shaky or solid, soldiers could stand firm or march forward to attack their target.

Our love affair with shoes includes infinite styles to complete our outfits, give us height, make our legs look good, or simply protect our feet. No matter what the reason is for all the attention, the shoe business is a multi-billion-dollar industry and many of us women don't mind contributing.

As Christ followers, our stylish sandals are designed for peace, made with the leather of the gospel. The gospel is the good news of Jesus's death and resurrection from the dead. He is alive in Heaven creating a pathway for us to God. Isn't that good news? Our peace is forged in our relationship with Jesus. No matter how unstable our situation, we are saved by Jesus Christ. We have the assurance of eternity with him. Our footing is firm as we stand on the foundation of peace.

One of the best techniques for helping anxious clients is called grounding. This method distracts us from our trigger to help us refocus on what is happening in the moment. There are many ways to do this, so feel free to search Google or check Pinterest to find one that feels most comfortable for you. A common method is to sit down or stand with your feet firmly planted on the ground. When a trigger takes you to the past, feeling the ground under your feet brings you back to the present, reminding you that there is no actual threat. Now, slowly breathe in God's peace, then exhale the pain of the past. Repeat until you feel safe and in control again.

No matter your favorite shoe type, always put on your stylish shoes of peace.

THE HANDBAG OF FAITH

"Hold up the shield of faith to stop the fiery arrows of the devil" (Ephesians 6:16).

In Biblical times, flaming arrows were the attack weapon of choice. The initial impact of the arrow hitting its target was detrimental enough, but the more devastating flames inflicted damage to everything nearby—the city walls, homes, animals, people. Sometimes the damage was beyond repair.

The Roman shield was not like the round shield carried by Captain America. Instead, it was shaped like a door, slightly curved in on both sides. The shield was four feet tall and 2½ feet wide, made of two pieces of wood covered with animal skin and linen soaked in water to be ready to extinguish the fiery arrows.

Here is the catch: the soldier had to have the shield with him for it to be effective. Just owning a shield meant nothing if the soldier did not carry it. As with the soldier, so it is with us. Our defensive weapon is useless if we don't carry it with us and use it.

I realize I may be stretching things a bit by comparing a handbag to a shield but go with me on this. Considering the number of things we women put in a purse and the weight we're carrying around, is it any wonder we see videos and news clips of women using their handbag as an effective shield and weapon? I'm just saying.

My sister, how many times are we caught defenseless when Satan sends his fiery arrows at our hearts and minds? We feel the initial blow, and the damage spreads like a fire through our spirit, leaving us devastated and struggling to recover as the sparks continue to burn. But when Satan's flame hits faith soaked in the water of the Word, the fire immediately goes out and no damage is incurred. God is even so good to us that he can and does repair even past damage that was able to penetrate our hearts and minds. Hallelujah!

Imagine the fiery arrows are darts of doubt designed to keep us feeling defeated when we experience a trigger. Soak yourself in the truth of God's Word, then when fear attacks, place your faith in that truth. That's how the shield works.

When the fiery arrow says, "I can't believe this is happening again," the shield of faith says, "But for you who fear my name, the Sun of Righteousness will rise with healing in his wings. And you will go free, leaping with joy like calves let out to pasture (Malachi 4:2).

When the fiery arrow says, "I can't take it anymore," the shield of faith says, "I pray that God, the source of hope, will fill you completely with joy and peace because you trust in him. Then you will overflow with confident hope through the power of the Holy Spirit (Romans 15:13).

When the fiery arrow says, "It will never get better," the shield of faith says, "So after you have suffered a little while, he will restore, support, and strengthen you, and he will place you on a firm foundation" (1 Peter 5:10).

Girl, can't you just hear the sizzle of the flame going out? Load up your handbag of faith with God's promises and don't ever leave home without it.

The Hat of Salvation

"Put on salvation as your helmet" (Ephesians 6:17).

Our next vital accessory is the helmet, or as I prefer to think of it, our hat of salvation. Roman soldiers wore iron helmets with cheek plates and neck guard to protect against penetrating sword blows. Bronze helmets proved ineffective against enemy attacks. With the stronger, more secure headgear, they marched into battle with confidence.

My sisters, our hats serve more than one purpose. Check out the various reasons for wearing a hat.

- as part of a uniform
- to protect the head
- to keep the head warm
- to act as a sunshade
- to indicate being part of a group
- to convey a message
- to show status
- for religious or political reasons
- to show ethnicity
- to attract attention
- to make one look taller
- to hide the hair or lack of it
- to accessorize an outfit

I didn't realize there were so many reasons to wear a hat! I usually wear one to look good. I guess being a native San Diegan, I don't think about needing to keep my head warm, but I understand heat escapes through our head, which is why hair is so important. A hat provides an extra layer of protection from the elements.

As Christians, our layer of protection comes with the knowledge of our salvation. We have protection from Satan's attacks as we live confidently in our position as members of God's family. We can legitimately tell all our enemies, "You do not want to mess with me, because I will go get my big brother Jesus, and tell my Daddy on you!" We can wear the hat of salvation with assurance that no matter what attacks come, we are not alone. Our Heavenly Family has our back and our head!

With your mind protected by the security of salvation, you have a choice when responding to triggers. Decide what you want to feel, then decide what you want to do. You don't have to push the pain away. Ask Jesus to help you. Shift your emotional state by going for a walk. Turn on your favorite music or sniff a calming essential oil like lavender. God wants you safe and protected by your hat of salvation.

THE PEPPER SPRAY OF THE WORD

"Take the sword of the Spirit, which is the word of God" (Ephesians 6:17).

While I was praying and asking the Holy Spirit to enlighten me about this familiar offensive weapon, he whispered to me before I could say amen. The sword is used to attack, but again, the soldier must pick it up. On top of that, he must practice using it before he enters the battle. No one in his right mind would pick up a weapon for the first time expecting to be able to use it flawlessly and understanding immediately how to handle it properly, which is why Roman centurions trained for many months.

These days, we may not be able to relate to swords as weapons, but we are probably more familiar with a weapon like pepper spray, one of the most effective defenses for women. When the hot, blinding liquid is sprayed into an attacker's eyes, a woman has time to flee or cry for help. The weapon can also be used from a distance, so she doesn't have to be close to her attacker. I have a friend who was a police officer. He told me that before he could use pepper spray, he had to learn everything about it. He studied the chemistry component and effects of the pepper spray and was even sprayed, so he experienced firsthand its potency. Training increased his skill and confidence with his weapon.

We, as Christians, forget the importance of studying and familiarizing ourselves with God's Word before attempting to utilize it for protection against our triggers. The Holy Spirit educates and equips us to use God's Word both defensively and offensively. But a weapon without practice is useless.

Jesus gives a beautiful example of swordplay when he is tempted in the wilderness by Satan. Jesus deflected every temptation Satan threw at him by using the sword of the Word, and the enemy left defeated. Powerful! Jesus did it and so can we.

Practice memorizing Scripture, so you are prepared when the attacks come. When you are feeling defeated and hopeless after a flashback, pull out the pepper spray of the Word and defend yourself. "The righteous person faces many troubles, but the Lord comes to the rescue each time" (Psalm 34:19). God promises to rescue you from your struggles every single time. "No one hates his own body but feeds and cares for it, just as Christ cares for the church" (Ephesians 5:29). Practice self-care by resting, getting exercise, and eating well. Avoid things that can trigger you like social media, music, crime shows, etc. Above all else, do not forget to practice the protection of the pepper spray of the Word of God. You will be glad you did.

THE BALM OF PRAYER

"Pray in the Spirit at all times and on every occasion. Stay alert and be persistent in your prayers" (Ephesians 6:18).

Technically, prayer is not listed in the spiritual armor. Yet a Roman soldier's armor becomes useless if he fails to stay alert, and the enemy attacks. There is no greater protection than continuous conversation with the One who cares about our wounded hearts. "If your heart is broken, you'll find God right there; if you're kicked in the gut, he'll help you catch your breath" (Psalm 34:18 MSG). He wants us to stay connected with him in his presence so he can take care of us amid our pain.

I got excited because Scripture tells us to be constantly in prayer. And I thought of something we women wear that surrounds us throughout the day. A balm is a fragrant ointment or lotion used to heal or soothe the skin. Occasionally, we put on more lotion after washing our dry hands. Even though we sometimes forget about the scent or no longer smell it, others do.

One night, when I kissed my daughter good night, she pointed at me and said, "You smell like my mommy." I was startled because it had been a long day, but she could still smell my favorite scented lotion even though I had not given it another thought after putting it on that morning. When we pray, sometimes we forget we told God about our hurts. We forget we asked him to heal us. We forget, but he does not. The aroma of our prayers surrounds us and floats toward Heaven. Look at these verses which connect scent to prayer:

"And when he took the scroll, the four living beings and the twenty-four elders fell down before the Lamb. Each one had a harp, and they held gold bowls filled with incense, which are the prayers of God's people" (Revelation 5:8).

"The smoke of the incense, mixed with the prayers of God's holy people, ascended up to God from the altar where the angel had poured them out" (Revelation 8:4).

Stay alert and apply the balm of prayer throughout the day. Praying and then having confidence in our God who hears and handles our prayers is the best offense and protection ever. Prayer is the last piece of our protective attire which will enable us to stand. We withstand the brown thread of triggers by being scented and protected with the balm of prayer.

Dressed for Success

Throughout this study of the armor of God, I can't help but see how God provides the armor but leaves it up to us to make it effective. Did you notice the various commands regarding each piece of our outfits? We are told to put on, hold up, and take—all actions we must perform. You know what this means? God does the impossible but leaves the possible for us to do. We get to cooperate with God in updating our defense system. My sister, when you get dressed in the morning, don't forget to arm yourself spiritually and mentally. Put on the body shaper of truth. Put on the bra of righteousness. Put on the shoes of peace. Hold up the handbag of faith. Put on the hat of salvation. Take the pepper spray of the Word. Smooth on the balm of prayer. Now, you are dressed for success. Now you are armed and dangerous, equipped and enabled to manage and defend against the brown warp thread of triggers.

ENDNOTES

CHAPTER ONE

1. "Children and Teens: Statistics," RAINN, accessed July 15, 2021, https://www.rainn.org/statistics/children-and-teens.
2. "Larry Nassar case: USA Gymnastics doctor 'abused 265 girls'," BBC News posted January 31, 2018, https://www.bbc.com/news/world-us-canada-42894833.
3. "More than 150 women testified at Larry Nassar's sentencing. Read what they had to say," The Morning Call, posted January 25, 2018, https://www.mcall.com/news/breaking/mc-nws-nassar-victims-gymnasts-speak-20180125-story.html.
4. The Morning Call, https://www.mcall.com/news/breaking/mc-nws-nassar-victims-gymnasts-speak-20180125-story.html.

CHAPTER TWO

1. Sarah Mallory, "Tapestries Report All the News that's Fit to Weave," The Metropolitan Museum of Art, accessed June 19, 2020, metmuseum.org/now-at-the-met/2014.
2. Sarah Mallory, "Making a Tapestry—How Did They Do That?" The Metropolitan Museum of Art, accessed June 19, 2020, http://www.metmuseum.org/blogs/now-at-the-met/2014/making-a-tapestry.

Chapter Three

1. *Diagnostic and Statistical Manual of Mental Disorders: DSM-5* (Arlington, VA: American Psychiatric Association, 2013), 271.
2. Maurizio and Zaya Benazzo, *The Wisdom of Trauma* (Sebastopol, CA: Science and Nonduality, 2021). https://thewisdomoftrauma.com/.
3. Christiane Sanderson, *Counseling Skills for Working with Trauma* (London: Jessica Kingsley Publishers, 2013), 17.

Chapter Five

1. Brené Brown, *Daring Greatly: How the Courage to Be Vulnerable Transforms the Way We Live, Love, Parent, and Lead* (New York: Penguin Random House, 2012), 68.
2. Brown, 71.

Chapter Six

1. "Building your resilience," American Psychological Association, accessed May 14, 2018, https://www.apa.org/helpcenter/road-resilience.
2. Jill Suttie, "Four Ways Social Support Makes You More Resilient," Greater Good Magazine, accessed May 14, 2018, https://greatergood.berkeley.edu/article/item/four_ways_social_support_makes_you_more_resilient.

Chapter Seven

1. Sue Johnson, *Hold Me Tight* (Boston, MA: Little, Brown Spark, 2008), 33-40.

Chapter Nine

1. J. P. Lange, P. Schaff, & W. G. T. Shedd, "A commentary on the Holy Scriptures: Mark" (Bellingham, WA: Logos Bible Software, 2008), 50

2. Carol Dweck, *Mindset: The New Psychology of Success* (New York: Random House, 2006), 6-10.

CHAPTER TEN

1. Dr. John D. Garr, *The Hem of His Garment: Touching the Power in God's Word* (Atlanta, GA: Golden Key Press, 2007), 49-66.

CHAPTER ELEVEN

1. Dr. E. James Wilder, Anna Kang, John Loppnow, Sungshim Loppnow, *Joyful Journey: Listening to Immanuel* (independently published on Amazon, 2020), 26.
2. "Speaking out from Within: Speaking Publicly About Sexual Assault," Resources, Pennsylvania Coalition Against Rape, https://pcar.org/sites/default/files/resource-pdfs/speaking_out_from_within-speaking_publicly_about_sexual_assault.pdf.

CHAPTER TWELVE

1. The Forgiveness Project, accessed April 10, 2019, www.theforgivenessproject.com.
2. Lysa TerKeurst, *Forgiving What You Can't Forget* (Nashville: Thomas Nelson, 2020), 43-44.
3. "The Deadly Consequences of Unforgiveness," News, CBN News, posted June 22, 2015, http://www1.cbn.com/cbnnews/healthscience/2015/June/The-Deadly-Consequences-of-Unforgiveness.

RESOURCES

SIGNS IT'S TIME TO SEEK A THERAPIST

1. If your experience with any of these emotions interferes with your relationships, work, or school:
    - Overwhelm
    - Anxiety
    - Depression
    - Apathy
    - Anger
    - Fatigue

2. If thinking about your issues consumes your thoughts
3. If the issue has diminished your quality of life
4. If nothing you have tried has worked for you
5. If family or friends suggest you go to therapy

HOW TO FIND THE RIGHT THERAPIST FOR YOU

1. Pray. Ask God to lead you to the therapist who is best equipped to help you with your problems. Don't start the search without Holy Spirit leading and directing you.
2. Word of Mouth. The best referrals come from someone you trust. Ask your family, friends, or pastor

3. Internet. Do a Google search for "Christian Therapist" or "Christian Counselor." If that is overwhelming, try these websites.
   - Focus on the Family https://www.focusonthefamily.com/get-help/counseling-services-and-referrals/.
   - Psychology Today https://www.psychologytoday.com/us/therapists/christian
   - The Christian Therapist Network https://www.christiantherapistnetwork.org/

4. Ask questions. When you find a therapist who may be a good fit for you, ask these questions during your complimentary consultation.
   - How many clients have you had with similar circumstances to my own?
   - Do you have specialized training with childhood sexual abuse?
   - How much do you charge? What are you sliding-scale options? Do you take insurance?

FURTHER READING

- *Rid of My Disgrace* by Justin S. Holcomb and Lindsey A. Holcomb (discussion guide available)
- *Journey to Heal: Seven Essential Steps of Recovery for Survivors of Childhood Sexual Abuse* by Crystal Sutherland.
- *Not Marked: Finding Hope and Healing after Sexual Abuse* by Mary DeMuth
- *Wounded Heart: Hope for Adult Victims of Childhood Sexual* Abuse by Dan Allender (workbook available)
- *Healing the Wounded Heart* by Dan Allender

- *On the Threshold of Hope: Opening the Door to Healing for Survivors of Sexual Abuse* by Diane Mandt Langberg, PhD (workbook available)
- *Suffering and the Heart of God: How Trauma Destroys and Christ Restores* by Diane Langberg, PhD
- *The Body Keeps the Score: Brain, Mind and Body in the Healing of Trauma* by Bessel van der Kolk, M.D.
- *From Pain to Power: Overcoming Sexual Trauma and Reclaiming Your True Identity* by Mary Ellen Mann
- *Healing for Damaged Emotions* by David A. Seamands (workbook available)
- *Breathe: Finding Freedom to Thrive in Relationships After Childhood Sexual Abuse* by Nicole Bromley
- *Hush: Moving from Silence to Healing After Childhood Sexual Abuse* by Nicole Bromley (workbook available)
- Hotlines
- Darkness to Light Sexual Assault Hotline: 866-367-5444
- RAINN (Rape Abuse & Incest National Network). Helps people affected by sexual violence: 800-656-HOPE
- National Child Abuse Hotline provides local referrals with the possibility of talking to a counselor. They provide service in over 140 languages: 800-4-A-CHILD (422.2253)

Videos

"I'm Not the Same," by Walter Hawkins https://youtu.be/mT6rDY4U2AU

"The Art of Making a Tapestry" by Getty Museum https://youtu.be/jIbu-dJuEho

"Walter Hawkins & Love Center Choir - When The Battle Is Over" https://youtu.be/P-8S9u9Ytn0

www.ingramcontent.com/pod-product-compliance
Lightning Source LLC
Chambersburg PA
CBHW060514090426
42735CB00011B/2217